DATE DUE

HANDBOOK OF RACIAL/ETHNIC MINORITY COUNSELING RESEARCH

HANDBOOK OF RACIAL/ETHNIC MINORITY COUNSELING RESEARCH

JOSEPH G. PONTEROTTO, Ph.D.

Associate Professor of Education
Coordinator, Counseling and Counseling Psychology Programs
Division of Psychological and Educational Services
Graduate School of Education
Fordham University at Lincoln Center
New York, New York

J. MANUEL CASAS, Ph.D.

Associate Professor of Education
Counseling Psychology Program
Department of Education
University of California at Santa Barbara
Santa Barbara, California

With a Foreword by
Derald Wing Sue, Ph.D.
Professor of Psychology
California State University, Hayward

CHARLES C THOMAS • PUBLISHER
Springfield • Illinois • U.S.A.

Published and Distributed Throughout the World by

CHARLES C THOMAS • PUBLISHER
2600 South First Street
Springfield, Illinois 62794-9265

© *1991 by* CHARLES C THOMAS • PUBLISHER

ISBN 0-398-05716-8

Library of Congress Catalog Card Number: 90-11292

With THOMAS BOOKS *careful attention is given to all details of manufacturing
and design. It is the Publisher's desire to present books that are satisfactory as to their
physical qualities and artistic possibilities and appropriate for their particular use.*
THOMAS BOOKS *will be true to those laws of quality that assure a good name
and good will.*

Printed in the United States of America
SC-R-3

Library of Congress Cataloging-in-Publication Data

Ponterotto, Joseph G.
   Handbook of racial/ethnic minority counseling research / Joseph G.
Ponterotto, J. Manuel Casas ; with a foreword by Derald Wing Sue.
     p. cm.
   Includes bibliographical references.
   Includes indexes.
   ISBN 0-398-05716-8
   1. Minorities—Counseling of—United States—Research. 2. Ethnic
groups—Counseling of—United States—Research.   I. Casas, J.
Manuel.   II. Title.
   [DNLM: 1. Counseling—methods. 2. Ethnic Groups. 3. Minority
Groups. 4. Racial Stocks. WA 305 P814h]
RC451.5.A2P66 1990
362.2'04256'08693—dc20
DNLM/DLC
for Library of Congress   90-11292
                                              CIP

To our mothers, Marion Ferrari Ponterotto and Elvira Casas; and in memory of our fathers, Italo Louis Ponterotto and Cruz Casas.

FOREWORD

We are quickly becoming a multicultural, multiracial, and multilingual society. Already 75 percent of those now entering the U.S. labor force are composed of women and minorities. The U.S. minority marketplace now equals the GNP of Canada, and demographers predict that by the time the so-called "baby boomers" retire, the majority of those contributing to the social security and pension plans of primarily white workers will be racial/ethnic minorities. Several states already (e.g., California) have greater than 50 percent racial/ethnic minority students in their public school systems. Because the fertility rate of white Americans is declining and the population of racial/ethnic minorities continues to grow (higher relative birthrates and immigration), racial/ethnic minorities will become the numerical majority some time in the next 30 years. These facts portend major changes in our educational, economic, social, and political systems.

As counselors and educators, we are faced with the inevitable challenge of cultural diversity. Unfortunately, the counseling profession has been remiss in addressing this issue. This is reflected in our graduate training programs and in our practice, where multicultural counseling continues to be neglected or inadequately presented. Most publications on the topic are either seriously deficient in covering this subject matter, or are a rehash of old ideas. Thus, it was a refreshing breath of air to discover such a well-written multicultural text. Even more gratifying to discover was how the authors tackled a traditionally difficult subject— cross-cultural research.

Ponterotto and Casas have chosen to strike out in a new direction and to accept the challenge of cultural diversity in their *Handbook of Racial/Ethnic Minority Counseling Research*. It not only represents a new direction for the counseling professions, but the book itself has no peers in the field. This is an extremely scholarly work which exemplifies the best in integrating research, theory, and practice devoted to racial/ethnic minorities. While others have written about minority research or cross-cultural psychology, this is the first exclusively research-focused text-book on racial/ethnic minority counseling. This is an up-to-date book which provides many valuable references for researchers interested in minority issues: university professors teaching research courses; and graduate students taking courses in counseling research. Indeed, this book would be of interest to any student, practitioner, or researcher interested in a scholarly overview of racial/ethnic minority counseling.

The organization of the text is superb. Each individual chapter builds on the previous one, allowing us to better understand how to conduct culturally-sensitive and meaningful research. Some of my reactions to the individual chapters are given below.

1. The first three chapters provide an excellent framework from which to understand research with racial/ethnic minority groups. Not only do the authors provide a strong rationale, but key terms are defined for the reader (majority group, white culture, race, etc.) allowing us to avoid the conceptual confusions which often occur in cross-cultural texts. The most up-to-date demographic projections and counts currently available are provided. The information in these three chapters alone would be useful in any counseling text on racial/ethnic minorities. Indeed, they may be important to include in any introductory counseling book as well.

2. Ponterotto and Casas do a fine job in tracing the full history of the American Psychological Association's and American Association for Counseling and Development's involvement in minority issues and concerns. Issues of cultural bias in theory and research are critically discussed and provide us with the conceptual basis for understanding racial/ethnic minority research.

3. More important are the authors' abilities to move beyond rhetoric in their chapters on research methodology and issues. They provide concrete examples of biased and unbiased research approaches, provide an organizational framework for analyzing recent research in racial/ethnic minority counseling, systematically examine culture-specific instruments currently in use, empirically discuss the validity of the most common criticisms directed at minority group research, and provide a unique, detailed coverage of both quantitative and qualitative research methods for use in cross-cultural counseling research.

4. Last, it is refreshing to see a research oriented book which is not negligent in discussing the moral, ethical, and social premises influencing racial/ethnic minority research. How to conduct relevant and respon-

sible research, and pointing to future racial/ethnic minority research directions were definite strengths.

In closing, this *Handbook* will be a major and substantive contribution to the counseling field. Joe Ponterotto and Manny Casas have done a much-needed service to the profession with their scholarly work and should be commended for their efforts. They will be imminently successful in their goal to provide readers with the necessary skills "to conduct culturally meaningful and helpful research."

Derald Wing Sue
Hayward, California

PREFACE

This *Handbook of Racial/Ethnic Minority Counseling Research* is precisely that—a handbook—a comprehensive guide to all aspects of counseling research with American racial/ethnic minority populations. This heavily referenced text includes coverage of research needs, topics, methods, issues, and ethics.

Despite the proliferation of racial/ethnic minority (or cross-cultural/ multicultural) focused counseling texts in the last two decades, the present book is the first to focus exclusively on research methods and procedures in racial/ethnic minority counseling. This *Handbook* is essentially a "how to" guide for conducting culturally sensitive, relevant, and meaningful counseling research with American racial/ethnic minority populations.

The demographic face of the United States is changing rapidly, and sometime during the 21st century racial/ethnic minority groups will become the nation's numerical majority. Counseling practitioners and researchers must be prepared for an increasingly diverse clientele in terms of race, ethnicity, cultural values, and language. To adequately service the mental health needs of a multicultural society, the counseling and psychology professions must first conduct systematic research to assess mental health needs and effective interventions across culturally diverse groups. Given that research forms the cornerstone for counseling theory and practice, it is clear that culturally relevant theories of behavior, and culturally responsive counseling interventions can only be developed after systematic research.

This book is organized along eleven chapters. Chapter One introduces the topic of racial/ethnic minority counseling research and provides a rationale for why and how this book could be of value to counseling and mental health researchers and practitioners. Chapter Two then profiles, in descriptive fashion, the major racial/ethnic minority groups constituting the focus of this book—Native Americans, Black or African Americans, Hispanic Americans, and Asian Americans/Pacific Islanders. Chapter

Two also presents definitions of important terms used throughout the text.

Chapter Three focuses exclusively on an in-depth examination of demographic trends in the United States. An accurate knowledge base of numerical, educational, and economic trends and projections among various racial/ethnic groups is essential for a clear understanding of the current and future mental health needs of an increasingly multicultural, multiracial, and multilingual society.

Chapter Four turns to a close look at the history of racial/ethnic minority counseling practice and research in the psychology and counseling professions. Knowledge of important events and trends of the American Psychological Association (APA) and the American Association for Counseling and Development (AACD) with regard to their multicultural focus, is an essential prerequisite to any student or scholar of racial/ethnic minority research.

In Chapter Five, extensive discussion is given to exposing the past, and often still present, cultural bias in counseling theory, practice, and research. Understanding cultural bias in counseling necessitates extensive knowledge of variant value systems, including that of the white middle class. Given the subtle, and sometimes hidden nature of ethnocentrism, this chapter relies heavily on specific examples demonstrating cultural bias in theory, practice, and research.

As a handbook, one goal of this book is to give counseling students and researchers easy and quick access to an extensive body of literature on racial/ethnic minority counseling. Chapter Six presents a topical review of recent conceptual and empirical counseling literature appearing in some of the counseling profession's most respected national journals. This chapter also presents a new conceptual model for placing research needs and foci into a holistic, coherent, and focused perspective.

With a topical breadth of multicultural knowledge in hand, Chapter Seven focuses specifically on methodology in racial/ethnic minority counseling research. This chapter identifies the ten most common criticisms directed at minority research, and then systematically determines which of these criticisms are actually supported by the data. The chapter concludes with specific suggestions for improving the future status of research methodology in the field.

Building on the findings presented in Chapter Seven, Chapters Eight and Nine detail, first, important quantitative procedures and instrumentation, and second, qualitative methods in racial/ethnic minority counseling research. A strong call is made by the authors to augment traditional quantitative research with varied qualitative methodologies. The multimethod research approach of carefully linking quantitative and qualitative methods in the same research programs are highlighted.

University-affiliated researchers in psychology and counseling have been harshly criticized by some members of racial/ethnic minority communities for conducting research primarily for their own professional benefits (e.g., to gain tenure and promotion) without really demonstrating a benevolent concern for the minority communities themselves. Chapter Ten presents a strong position on the researcher's ethical and professional responsibility to bring the results of her or his research back to the community in some form. This chapter talks at length about how researchers and universities can better collaborate with racial/ethnic minority communities.

Chapter Eleven briefly summarizes the content highlighted in previous chapters and then presents twelve specific directions for needed research in the racial/ethnic minority counseling area. These research suggestions represent a coherent integration of many of the issues raised in previous chapters. The major purpose of Chapter Eleven, and to some degree the book in general, is to stimulate among students and scholars interest and activity in racial/ethnic minority counseling research. Our goal in this text has been to equip the reader with the necessary sensitivity, skills, directions, and ethical philosophy necessary to conduct culturally meaningful and helpful research.

Joseph G. Ponterotto
J. Manuel Casas

CONTENTS

HANDBOOK OF RACIAL/ETHNIC MINORITY COUNSELING RESEARCH

Chapter One

INTRODUCTION: CURRENT STATUS OF RACIAL/ETHNIC MINORITY COUNSELING PRACTICE AND RESEARCH

As a collective group, racial/ethnic minority populations in the United States—namely Blacks, Hispanics, Asian American/Pacific Islanders, and Native Americans—are growing in numbers at a much faster rate than the White majority population. By the year 2,000, racial/ethnic minority populations will constitute 30 percent of the total U.S. population; and sometime during the 21st century, the current White majority will become the nation's numerical minority group (Wilson & Gutierrez, 1985). As minority groups continue to grow in numbers their concurrent mental health needs will expand, and counseling professionals will be increasingly called upon to provide culturally relevant services.

This chapter introduces the reader to three important issues in the field of racial/ethnic minority counseling: (a) the need for a racial/ethnic minority perspective in counseling; (b) the current status of racial/ethnic minority focused counseling practice, training, and research; and (c) future perspectives for racial/ethnic minority counseling research.

NEED FOR A RACIAL/ETHNIC MINORITY PERSPECTIVE IN COUNSELING

Clearly, one of the most important topics in counseling and counseling psychology today is racial/ethnic minority focused (or multicultural) counseling. In a recent editorial of the *Journal of Multicultural Counseling and Development*, the journal's editor, Courtland Lee (1989), noted:

It is apparent to me that multicultural counseling is presently the hottest topic in the profession. Every sector of the profession seems to be searching for new ways to intervene successfully into the lives of people from increasingly diverse client populations. This would seem natural because American society in the last several decades has become more pluralistic and projections suggest that

3

ethnic minority groups will have an even greater impact on population demographics in the next century (p. 2).

Speaking among a panel of multicultural experts at a recent conference of the American Psychological Association, Paul Pedersen (in Ponterotto, Atkinson, Casas, Oda, & Pedersen, 1987) equated the approaching impact of the multicultural counseling movement with that previously created by the psychodynamic, behavioral, and humanistic movements in counseling. In his conference address, Pedersen depicted the current multicultural emphasis as psychology's "Fourth Force." More recently, Pedersen (1988) further specified his view, noting that:

> It seems likely, therefore, that the current trend toward multicultural awareness among counselors will have as great an impact on the helping professions in the next decade as Roger's "third force" of humanism had on the prevailing psychodynamic and behavioral systems (p. vii).

There is little doubt that as the population demographics of the United States continues to change at a rapid pace, the emphasis in and need for culturally pluralistic counseling approaches will intensify. Fortunately, the counseling profession has begun to address the issue of cultural diversity in counseling (Casas, 1984). Hollis and Wantz (1986) note that one of the fastest growing courses (in terms of new offerings) across counseling training programs nationwide, is in the area of multicultural or racial/ethnic minority counseling. An assessment of chronologically-ordered curriculum surveys conducted in 1976 (McFadden & Wilson, 1977), in 1985 (Ibrahim, Stadler, Arredondo, & McFadden, 1986), in 1988 (Strozier & Hills, 1989), and in 1989 (Hills & Strozier, 1990) document the increasing number of programs including multicultural courses as part of the core counseling curriculum. In the most recent survey, Hills and Strozier (1990) found that 88 percent of the programs now offer a multicultural-focused course, and 59 percent require at least one such course.

Professional counseling organizations such as the American Psychological Association's (APA) Division of Counseling Psychology, and the American Association for Counseling and Development (AACD), and its particular subdivision—the Association for Multicultural Counseling and Development (AMCD), are beginning to take more active stands on the status of racial/ethnic minority counseling training and research (Gazda, Rude, & Weissberg, 1988; Lee, 1989; Parker, 1988; Pedersen, 1988). These professional organizations are calling for increased and culturally-sensitized training and research efforts relative to America's racial/ethnic minority groups. Considering recent and projected demographic shifts (Acosta-Belen & Sjostrom, 1988; Hodgkinson, 1985) [demographics will be covered in Chapter Three] as well as recent legal and affirmative action trends (Ponterotto, Lew, & Bullington, in press), it is becoming a well-accepted fact in the counseling profession that the field of racial/ethnic minority or multicultural counseling will become increasingly important to the counseling profession and to the practicing counselor.

CURRENT STATUS OF RACIAL/ETHNIC MINORITY-FOCUSED COUNSELING PRACTICE, TRAINING, AND RESEARCH

In the last two decades the counseling profession has devoted increased attention to the mental health status and needs of racial/ethnic minority groups (Casas, 1984; Ponterotto & Sabnani, 1989). Yet, despite this increased attention, the field of racial/ethnic minority counseling, or multicultural (or cross-cultural) counseling as it is often known, is still considered to be relatively young and in its infancy (Heath, Neimeyer, & Pedersen, 1988; Pedersen, 1985, 1988). It is clear that as the racial/ethnic populations continue to grow at a much faster rate than the white majority group, the counseling service and research needs of these groups will increase concurrently (Casas, 1984; Ponterotto & Casas, 1987; President's Commission on Mental Health, 1978).

Notwithstanding the counseling profession's recent interest in and commitment to quality racial/ethnic minority-focused counseling services, many minority scholars are quite critical of the fact that the counseling profession is not doing enough to meet the growing needs of a rapidly expanding population. Numerous writers (e.g., Casas, 1984, 1985a; Pedersen, 1985, 1988; D.W. Sue, 1981; D.W. Sue & D. Sue, in press) in the counseling field note that much remains to be done before racial/ethnic minority clientele receive the quality of counseling services currently being administered to the White majority group in the United States.

First, critics argue that the majority of traditionally-trained counselors operate from a culturally-biased and encapsulated framework (Parker, 1988; Pedersen, 1988; Wrenn, 1962, 1985) which results in the provision of culturally conflicting and even oppressive counseling treatments (Ponterotto & Benesch, 1988; D.W. Sue, 1981). These counselors, although well-intentioned and well-meaning, often and unknowingly impose their White middle-class value system on to culturally different clients who may possess alternative and equally meaningful and justifiable value orientations (Katz, 1985; Ponterotto & Benesch, 1988; D.W. Sue, 1981). Second, counseling training programs are considered by many (e.g., Atkinson, Morten, & D.W. Sue, 1989; Katz, 1985; D.W. Sue, 1981) to be proponents of the status quo. These programs and their faculty, the critics argue, continue to teach counselors out of traditional, Western European influenced, training models. Thus white, middle-class male perceptions of normal and appropriate behavior are set as the standard from which to judge, diagnose, and treat all clients (Pedersen, 1987, 1988). As long as training models continue to be, for the most part, culturally-biased, the graduates of these programs will continue to operate from a biased perspective. Third, a number of multicultural scholars have harshly criticized the status of counseling research directed toward racial/ethnic minority groups (e.g., Casas, 1985a; D.W. Sue, 1981; see also S. Sue, 1988; S. Sue & Zane, 1987). Given that research is the cornerstone of and forms the foundation for counseling training and practice, it is appropriate to cover this third area in a bit more detail.

Perhaps the strongest criticism leveled at the status of racial/ethnic minority counseling focuses on inadequate and culturally-biased research efforts (Casas, 1985a; Casas, Ponterotto, & Gutierrez, 1986; Ponterotto, 1988b; D.W. Sue, 1981). The main concern here is that culturally-insensitive research fosters and further perpetuates inadequate training models and subsequent counseling services. Without quality, culturally-relevant and meaningful research, the status of minority mental health counseling has little chance of witnessing significant improvement. Casas (1985a) summarizes criticisms directed towards the present status of racial/ethnic minority focused research efforts; his major points are paraphrased below.

1. The research has employed conceptually-biased research paradigms that address minorities from a pathological, deviant, and culturally-deficient perspective.
2. Much of the research has been anecdotal in nature, offering interesting speculations without the support of empirical data.
3. Research has examined specific client/counselor variables that are believed to impact the counseling process (e.g., client attitudes, client-counselor racial similarity), but it has virtually ignored impor-

tant intrapersonal and extrapersonal factors such as communication styles, acculturation, and discrimination and poverty, that may give shape and meaning to the minority person's behavior.

4. Research has neglected to consider and study the tremendous heterogeneity existing in racial/ethnic minority populations, and has as a result, further fostered and perpetuated ethnic stereotypes and global categorizations.
5. Past counseling research has relied too heavily on analogue studies that tend to select easily accessible subject populations (e.g., college students) that may not be very representative of the larger community.

These five criticisms of racial/ethnic minority focused counseling research expressed by Casas (1985a) are but just a few of the many appearing in recent literature. Chapter Seven is devoted entirely to identifying and either validating or disputing major research criticisms. At this point, however, it is important to turn our attention to some important research needs in the field.

FUTURE PERSPECTIVES ON RACIAL/ETHNIC MINORITY COUNSELING RESEARCH

At the Third National Conference for Counseling Psychology (see Gazda, Rude, & Weissberg, 1988), a distinguished panel of research experts (Gelso, Betz, Friedlander, Helms, Hill, Patton, Super, & Wampold, 1988) identified three important areas for further research in the area of racial/ethnic minority counseling. The three points of concern were posited as recommendations and are quoted below.

1. At a simple quantitative level, a greater amount of scientific work is needed in the areas of multi- and cross-cultural counseling psychology. Theory development and testing are called for as regards cross-cultural interactions, and research is needed on the applicability of general theories to cross-cultural and minority situations. In all of the scientific work that is done, careful attention must be given to terminology and to the definitions that are used, for example of minority group status, race, ethnicity, culture, cross-cultural counseling, and so on (p. 398).
2. Although research approaches of all kinds can be valuable, there is a great need for studies of actual interventions in the cross-cultural

area (as opposed to studies done in the laboratory and analogues of actual interventions). A balance of laboratory and field research is needed, and that balance will be attained by a relative increase in research on actual counseling (p. 398).

3. Researchers and evaluators of research need to be more open to nontraditional research approaches, especially with regard to sampling and sample size. If we are to get more research on multi- and cross-cultural issues as they operate in the real world of counseling, research evaluators must be more amenable to case study approaches and other small sample procedures (p. 398).

Another set of important suggestions was proffered by Suinn (1985) in his contribution to a special issue of *The Counseling Psychologist* (edited by Smith & Vasquez, 1985) devoted to "Cross-Cultural Counseling." Suinn emphasized that what the counseling profession needs now is "A handbook of ethnic research methodology." Important ingredients of the ideal handbook would include (a) clear definitions of the terms being used and the populations being studied; (b) a delineation of procedures for assessing one's sample and gaining participant cooperation; (c) consideration of potentially powerful variables to study, as well as the identification of culturally-irrelevant variables; and (d) the careful discussion of instrumentation selection, use, and interpretation.

This *Handbook of Racial/Ethnic Minority Counseling Research* is intended to fill the profession's strong need, as highlighted above by Suinn (1985), for a definitive research text in the racial/ethnic minority counseling area. This book addresses the concerns expressed by Suinn (1985), and it also presents mechanisms and procedures for operationalizing and putting into action the specific recommendations put forth by Gelso et al. (1988). As already noted, one of the first important steps in conceptualizing and conducting research with culturally-varied groups is to understand the target population, and be familiar with the most accurate terminology used to describe this population. To this end, Chapter Two presents some important definitions and descriptive cultural profiles.

Chapter Two

RACIAL/ETHNIC MINORITY POPULATIONS: DEFINITIONS AND DESCRIPTIVE PROFILES

As highlighted at the end of Chapter One, an important first step in interpreting and conducting counseling research on racial/ethnic minority populations is to have an accurate understanding of the definitions with which you are working and the populations which you are studying. One problem in the minority research area is that numerous terminologies have been incorporated by various writers to discuss the same topics (Gelso et al., 1988). This lack of consistency in the literature has created a great deal of confusion for the scholar and student of minority-based research. Therefore, the first major section of Chapter Two is devoted to defining and clarifying important terms that will be used throughout the book.

The second section of Chapter Two then provides brief descriptive profiles of the four racial/ethnic minority groups—Native Americans, Black or African Americans, Hispanic Americans, and Asian American/Pacific Islanders—constituting the focus of this book. Chapter Three then presents a comprehensive demographic profile of these four groups including present and future growth projections, current educational status, and present economic conditions.

CLARIFICATION OF TERMS

Race

For our purposes, race refers to a *biological* classification system determined by physical characteristics. Krogman's (1945) definition of race is most appropriate:

> A subgroup of peoples possessing a definite combination of physical characters, of genetic origin, the combination of which to varying degrees distinguishes the sub-group from other sub-groups of mankind [womenkind] (p. 49).

9

Among the most commonly recognized physical characteristics that distinguish races of people are skin pigmentation, head form, nasal index, lip form, facial index, stature, and the color distribution and texture of body hair (see Simpson & Yinger, 1985). Although race is often used as a social mechanism to categorize people, Atkinson, Morten, and D.W. Sue (1979) stress that there are many more similarities than differences among races, and that, in fact, there are more differences within racial groups than between them.

It is important to emphasize that a number of writers have expressed concern over the social interpretation of the term "race." d'Ardenne and Mahtani (1990) note that in everyday terminology, "race" usually refers to differences in skin color and is often used in a derogatory manner. These authors note that the biological emphasis on race is fraught with complexity and contradiction due to the interaction of social, political, and cultural factors. Phillips and Rathwell (1986) believe that the study of race has more to do with social interactions and power than with mere biological differences (see related discussions by Atkinson et al. [1989] and Dominelli [1988]).

Ethnicity

Race should not be confused with ethnicity, which has no biological or genetic foundation (Atkinson et al., 1979). Rose (1964) defines ethnicity as a group classification of individuals who share a unique social and cultural heritage (e.g., language, religion, custom) passed on from generation to generation. Using more specific terms, Yinger (1976) defines an "ethnic group", as:

A segment of a larger society whose members are thought, by themselves and/or others, to have a common origin and to share important segments of a common culture and who, in addition, participate in shared activities in which the common origin and culture are significant ingredients (p. 200).

The distinction between ethnicity and race can be clarified through a specific example: Jews, given their shared social, cultural, and religious heritage are an ethnic group; they are not, however, a race (Thompson & Hughes, 1958).

Culture

The term "culture" has been frequently misunderstood and misused. "Culture" is often used in the literature as synonymous with race and ethnicity, however, as Moore (1974) points out:

> Sometimes we tend to confuse race and ethnic groups with culture. Great races do have different cultures. Ethnic groups within races differ in cultural context. But, people of the same racial origin and of the same ethnic groups differ in their cultural matrices. All browns, or blacks, or whites, or yellows, or reds are not alike in the cultures in which they live and have their being (p. 41).

A succinct definition of "culture" is offered by Linton (1945), who describes culture as:

> ... The configuration of learned behavior whose components and elements are shared and transmitted by the members of a particular society (p. 32). As Atkinson et al. (1979) point out: It is clear that the various ethnic groups within racial and among racial categories have their own unique cultures. It should also be clear that even within ethnic groups, small groups of individuals may develop behavior or patterns they share and transmit, which in essence constitute a form of culture (p. 5).

Minority

Our usage of the term "minority" throughout this text parallels that coined by Wirth (1945):

> A group of people who, because of physical or cultural characteristics, are singled out from others in society in which they live for differential and unequal treatment, and who therefore regard themselves as objects of collective discrimination ... Minority status carries with it the exclusion from full participation in the life of the society (p. 347).

It is important to note that when conceptualizing the term "minority," we are not speaking in terms of a numerical minority, although the racial/ethnic minority groups to be focused on in this text are currently and for the next few decades numerical minorities. More crucial to our definition of "minority" is restriction in terms of educational, economic, and political opportunities. A minority group is essentially one that is oppressed either overtly or subtly by the majority society.

Majority

The sheer existence of "minority groups" in the United States presupposes the existence of a "majority group." The majority group in the United States is the group that holds the balance of economic and political power. It is that group whose cultural value system is deemed by its members to be the model value system, the one to be emulated (majority and minority value systems will be discussed at length in Chapter Five). Undoubtedly, the mainstream majority group in the United States is that composed of White, Anglo-Saxon Protestants (also known by the acronym—WASPS). As Gordon (1964) aptly notes:

> If there is anything in American life which can be described as an overall American culture which serves as a reference point for immigrants and their children, it can best be described . . . as the middle-class cultural patterns of largely White Protestant, Anglo-Saxon origins (cited in Markides & Mindel, 1987, p. 14).

Our conception of the White majority is not confined to White Anglo-Saxon Protestants, but includes all white ethnic groups in the United States. Clearly, from a minority perspective, the majority culture consists of all non-Black, non-Hispanic, non-Asian (or Indian) groups. For example, when an American Indian is referring to the "White man," she or he is referring to all white-skinned people, not just White Anglo-Saxon Protestants. Similarly, Blacks perceive all White people (including, at times, some Hispanics) as part of the dominant white system (see Markides & Mindel, 1987). Thus our conception and usage of the term "White majority culture" includes all Whites in America, including Italian Americans, Jewish Americans, Polish Americans, Irish Americans, etc.

It is important to note that although most White immigrant groups received their share of prejudice and oppression when first arriving in America, their situation and experience in the United States cannot, in our opinion, be equated with the historical and continuing oppression faced by people of color (see Simpson & Yinger, 1985). Because of their more Anglo features (mainly white skin), White ethnics were allowed eventually (sometimes by changing their last name) to assimilate and become part of "mainstream" America. People of color, however, because of their physical differences, have not been allowed by the majority to fully assimilate into the "land of opportunity."

The definition of "White culture" that we use throughout this text is echoed by Katz (1985):

> White culture is the synthesis of ideas, values, and beliefs coalesced from descendants of White European ethnic groups in the United States (p. 617).

Racial/Ethnic Minority Groups

This book is about counseling research with four groups that have been deemed as meriting special attention by such professional organizations as the National Institute of Mental Health (NIMH), the American Psychological Association (APA), and the American Association for Counseling and Development (AACD) [Casas, 1984]: Native Americans (including American Indians, Eskimos, and Aleuts), Black Americans, Hispanic Americans, and Asian Americans/Pacific Islanders. Each of these groups will be briefly profiled in the next section of this chapter.

Although at various points throughout this book, specific research endeavors will be discussed in relation to the groups individually, when referring to the groups collectively the term "racial/ethnic minority" groups will be used. *Racial* incorporates the biological/hereditary classification—specifically Mongoloid (Asian American/Pacific Islander and Native Americans), Negroid (Black Americans), and Caucasoid (White Americans). Note that Hispanics, depending on their point of geographical origin can be representative of any of these three races (see Casas, 1984; U.S. Census, 1987). *Ethnic* is a group classification of individuals who share a unique social and cultural heritage. *Minority* incorporates the lower (educational, economic, and political) status conferred upon particular groups by the White majority culture.

Our usage of the term "racial/ethnic minority counseling" is in line with the term "cross-cultural counseling," often the preferred terminology in the counseling literature (see for example, Pedersen, 1985; Smith & Vasquez, 1985). This latter term, however, is open to numerous interpretations which according to Casas (1984) and Pedersen (1978) could include any dyadic encounter in which the counselor and client are culturally different. Thus sex, age, lifestyle, and socioeconomic status differences would all constitute cross-cultural counseling. Moreover, "cross-cultural" may also encompass counseling and research which is cross-national or international in focus (Casas, 1984). Thus for reasons of accuracy and clarity, "racial/ethnic minority" is the most precise umbrella term to describe the four major groups constituting the focus of this book. Working from this perspective, attention is now directed to a brief descriptive profile on each of these groups.

RACIAL/ETHNIC MINORITY GROUP PROFILES

Native Americans

It is appropriate to begin our brief discussion of racial/ethnic group profiles with Native Americans—the true "original" Americans. Native American groups include American Indians, Eskimos, and Aleuts (Alaska natives). Most of the empirical counseling literature on Native Americans has focused on the American Indian, and thus we will focus our brief descriptive profile on this culturally-diverse and heterogeneous group. The reader interested in specific information on Alaska Natives is referred to Dinges, Trimble, Manson, and Pasquale (1981), and Manson (1982).

American Indians are geographically dispersed throughout the United States. Citing the work of Manson and Trimble (1982), LaFromboise (1988) emphasizes the heterogeneity existing within the American Indian population. She notes that there are some 511 federally-recognized Native entities and an additional 365 state-recognized American Indian tribes. Further, approximately 200 distinct tribal languages are spoken today among the American Indian population. To categorize or stereotype a "typical" American Indian is not possible nor desirable. Counseling practitioners and researchers must acknowledge and be sensitive to the tremendous heterogeneity and diversity existing among the American Indian people (see discussions by Herring, 1989, 1990).

The 1980 national census reported the American Indian population to number roughly 1.5 million, almost double the 1970 estimate (U.S. Department of Commerce, 1983). A more recent estimate (LaFromboise & Low, 1989) places the current American Indian population between 1.5 and 1.8 million, which as explained in Chapter Three is a gross underestimate of this population. States with relatively high American Indian populations include California, Oklahoma, Arizona, New Mexico, North Carolina, and Alaska (Dillard, 1985). American Indians are becoming increasingly urbanized, moving to cities both for subsistence and gainful employment. The last national census (1980) documented that only

24 percent of the American Indian population lived on reservations (LaFromboise, 1988).

The American Indian population is remarkably young; with a median age of 20.4 years (Alaska Natives median age = 17.9 years). This figure stands in sharp and significant contrast to the total U.S. population median age which stands at 30.3 years (LaFromboise, 1988). [Refer to Chapter Three for more detailed age-related comparisons across racial/ethnic groups.]

The mental health research and service needs of American Indians and other Native American groups are great. The historical and con—tinuing mistreatment of American Indians need not be discussed here. Suffice it to say that this group has been the object of continued oppression, discrimination, prejudice, violence, misunderstanding, and stereotyping (see Banks, 1984; Markides & Mindel, 1987). In terms of educational, economic, and political power, American Indians are at the lowest ends of the spectrum; more often than not, they have little influence over what happens in America or in their own lives.

American Indian poverty levels, unemployment, malnutrition, inade-quate health care, shortened life expectancy, and substance abuse and suicide rates (among some tribes), all constitute important research topics for the counselor. Equally important areas for research include studying the dominant White culture's behavior (including attitudes, feelings, misunderstanding) towards American Indian populations.

Black Americans

Black Americans or African Americans, which for a growing number of persons from this racial group is a preferred term, constitute the nation's largest racial/ethnic minority group. Currently numbering close to 30 million, Blacks represent 12.1 percent of the total U.S. population. Further, the Black population is growing at a faster pace than the white majority with an annual growth rate of 1.8 percent, as compared to only a 0.06 percent growth rate for Whites [Hispanic annual growth rate is the highest at 6.1%] (Malgady, Rogler, & Costantino, 1987). Blacks are found living and working throughout the entire United States; with their projected 1990 geographical dispersion as follows: Northeast, 11.3 percent; Midwest, 10.0 percent; South, 18.8 percent; and West, 5.6 percent (U.S. Census Bureau of the Census, 1988).

The Black experience in America is unique. This group first arrived in the United States in the 1600s, and of course, unlike immigrant groups who followed, they came involuntarily as slaves. Stripped of their land, families, languages, and cultural heritages, Americans of African descent have shown remarkable strength and resiliency in their striving to become fully valued, appreciated, and accepted Americans.

As with the other racial/ethnic groups discussed in this chapter, Black Americans are a very heterogeneous group. Blacks as a racial group are represented by numerous and diverse ethnic and cultural groups, including Spanish-speaking Blacks from Cuba, Puerto Rico, and Panama, among others; Blacks from the various Caribbean Islands, from Northern Europe, and American Indian Blacks (see Allen, 1988; Baker, 1988; McKenzie, 1986). It is important for counselors to acknowledge and understand the tremendous diversity within the Black population in the United States. One's view of his or her blackness and one's racial identity commitment are important variables in the counseling process (see Helms, 1990; Parham, 1989; White & Parham, 1990).

Despite many within-group (intracultural) differences among the Black population, the group as a whole, because of their darker skin, has been subjected to continuing majority-group oppression. In no case has the sheer brutality and evil of racism, prejudice, and penetrating hate been so evident and salient as in the White majority's treatment of Blacks throughout U.S. history. The long-term effects of historical oppression coupled with present life circumstances which generally include lower educational and economic achievement, predispose many Blacks to high levels of psychological stress. All counseling and mental health agencies and organizations emphasize that the counseling profession must devote increased attention and improved services to Black Americans.

Hispanic Americans

Hispanics are a tremendously diverse group, composed of numerous subgroups, including Mexican Americans, Puerto Ricans, Cuban Americans, South and Central Americans, among others. In addition to the marked cultural diversity reflected between these specific subgroups, there is also a great deal of heterogeneity within each specific subgroup. For instance, as a result of the acculturation process, Mexican Americans who recently arrived in the U.S. from Mexico may be quite different in values, behaviors, attitudes, and counseling needs than Mexican Americans who are third generation Americans. Further within-group diversity among Mexican Americans is also attributable to geographical region and socioeconomic status.

Overall, Hispanics represent the fastest growing racial/ethnic group in the United States. Currently, in total numbers, Hispanics are the second largest minority group, behind Black Americans. In March of 1987, there were 18.8 million Hispanics in the United States (7.9% of the total population). This figure represents a 30 percent increase over the 1980 census figure of 14.5 million (then 6.4% of the total population). During this same seven-year period the growth rate for non-Hispanics was 6.0 percent. Again, as with the Native American these statistics represent a gross underestimate of this population. More information relative to this point is provided in Chapter Three.

Of the many Hispanic groups in the United States, the Central and South Americans experienced the greatest growth rate during the 1982–1987 period—40 percent; whereas Cuban Americans experienced the slowest growth—7 percent. Given the overall high growth rate of Hispanics in general, it is expected that by the year 2035, they will surpass Blacks as the largest racial/ethnic minority group in the United States.

Hispanics of Mexican origin are clearly the largest Hispanic subgroup, accounting for 63 percent of the total Hispanic population. Representation among other Hispanic subgroups are as follows: Puerto Ricans at 12 percent, Central and South Americans at 11 percent, Cubans at 5 percent, and "other Hispanics" who listed census identification labels such as Spanish, Spanish American, and Latino (this group includes many Hispanics (probably of Mexican origin) from the Southwest, especially New Mexico) at 8 percent (National Council of La Raza, 1987).

Although Hispanics are geographically dispersed throughout the United States, particular groups can be found in higher concentrations in some areas. Specifically, a majority of the Mexican Americans reside in the Southwest. Puerto Ricans reside primarily in and around New York City. A majority of Cuban Americans live in South Florida and in the vicinity of New York City. A number of Central American groups are locating particularly in the New York City area, Los Angeles, and San Francisco. It should be emphasized that the Hispanic groups are growing in numbers so rapidly that it is difficult through census counts to keep track of their national migration. Many large numerical pockets of South and Central Americans, for example, can now be found in the South and Midwest.

Demographic studies indicate that overall, the Hispanic population is younger, less educated, poorer, and more likely to live in inner-city neighborhoods than the general population (Rogler, Malgady, Costantino, & Blumenthal, 1987). These life stressors, coupled with their linguistic minority status (Malgady, Rogler, & Costantino, 1987), make Hispanics particularly vulnerable to psychological problems requiring counseling services.

Asian Americans/Pacific Islanders

Like Hispanics, Asian Americans/Pacific Islanders are represented by a number of major subgroups, including Japanese, Chinese, Filipino, Koreans, Guamians, Malays, Samoans, and Southeast Asians. An umbrella term used to identify these groups collectively is "Asian American/Pacific Islander." At present, this collective, heterogeneous group represents the third largest racial/ethnic minority group in the United States. In 1980, they numbered approximately 3.5 million. Asian American groups are growing in rapid numbers, and some projections expect this total population in the year 2,000 to number over 9.8 million (see data summarized by Nagata, 1989).

Chinese and Japanese were the first Asians to settle in the United States in large numbers, and like other Asian and Hispanic groups, they arrived in the hopes of improving their economic conditions, lifestyles, and social and political life (Dillard, 1985). Filipino immigrants came to the United States after the Chinese and Japanese, and they arrived in large numbers in the 1920s when immigration laws restricted the number of Japanese and Mexican laborers. Vietnamese and other Southeast Asian groups (Laotians, Cambodians) are more recent immigrants (actually *refugees*) to the United States, arriving in large numbers after the fall of Saigon to North Vietnam in 1975. Unlike the early Asian immigrant groups who arrived in the United States to pursue a "better life," Southeast Asian refugees have been coming to the United States to "save" their lives. Many of these individuals were fleeing from war, hunger, and a marked oppression.

Asian American/Pacific Islanders are dispersed throughout the United States. A large percentage are located in urban areas in large cities on the

West and East coasts. As immigrant, foreign language, people of color, all Asian American/Pacific Islander groups have had a challenging adjustment to life and.work in the United States. All have been objects of past and continued racism and prejudice. Although some Asian American/Pacific Islander groups have been portrayed as "model minorities" in terms of significant educational and economic success, it must be emphasized that large percentages of these groups live in poverty and suffer high levels of psychological stress (see Banks, 1984; D.W. Sue & D. Sue, 1985).

Asian American/Pacific Islander groups are tremendously diverse. Like the Hispanics in America, Asian American/Pacific Islanders differ markedly from subgroup to subgroup. Further, within a particular subgroup, varying levels of acculturation attest to marked within-group heterogeneity. For instance, a third generation Japanese American youth may be more similar to a white friend in terms of values, attitudes, and cultural behaviors than to his/her grandfather or same-age cousin who just arrived from Japan. The tremendous heterogeneity both between and within various Asian American/Pacific Islander groups defies categorization and stereotypic description.

In regards to this collective racial/ethnic minority group, one important point is clear: they have been subjects of continuing societal oppression, discrimination, and misunderstanding, and are in need of culturally-relevant counseling research and service.

CONCLUSION

This chapter has introduced important terms and descriptive profiles that should be kept in mind when reading subsequent chapters. In closing this chapter it is important to summarize and emphasize four points. First, racial/ethnic minority populations are growing at a much faster rate that the White majority population. This disproportionate growth is due primarily to higher fertility rates and continuing immigration trends (both legal and illegal) among some segments of the minority populations. Second, as the minority populations continue to grow and continue to face societal (e.g., misunderstanding, discrimination, and prejudice) and personal (e.g., managing the culture shock experience, including learning a new language [in some cases]) obstacles to full participation in American life (see special report, One-Third of a Nation,

1988), they will experience increasing psychological stress requiring appropriate counseling intervention. Third, it goes without saying that to improve the quantity and quality of services delivered to racial/ethnic minority populations, increased and sensitized research efforts aimed at more fully understanding the psychological stressors, mental health needs, and preferred intervention modalities of these groups is needed.

Chapter Three

RACIAL/ETHNIC MINORITY POPULATIONS: A COMPREHENSIVE DEMOGRAPHIC PROFILE

As highlighted in Chapters One and Two, the "demographic face" of America is undergoing a rapid transformation. Persons from diverse racial/ethnic minority groups are growing at a faster pace than the White majority, and they are becoming increasingly visible in the community and in the counselor's office. Given this scenario, there is no question that counselors need to have an accurate understanding of the demographic characteristics of the populations they will be serving (Casas, 1984).

Given the emerging status of racial/ethnic minority counseling training, it is a well accepted fact that the majority of practicing counselors were not adequately trained to understand and in turn effectively meet the mental health needs of non-White, nonmiddle-class persons. Consequently, it is safe to say that lacking such training, a significant number of counselors, and White middle-class counselors in particular, are practicing outside the limits of their training and competence. Needless to say, given existing professional ethical guidelines (for details relative to this issue, refer to Chapter Ten), such practice borders on unethical behavior. To rectify this situation, a first step that all counselors must take is to acquire an accurate understanding of the demographic traits and patterns that are characteristic of the major racial/ethnic minority groups in the United States.

Sensitive to this perspective, the purpose of this chapter is to provide the reader with a concise yet comprehensive overview of the most recent demographic statistics available relative to the major racial/ethnic groups in the United States. The chapter is organized along three major sections that address major factors that have direct implications for the provision of counseling services to racial/ethnic minority populations. The first section discusses population demographics and covers present and projected growth patterns, age categorizations, and current fertility rates.

21

The second section focuses on educational data and covers general school completion rates, present enrollments in higher education, minority student attrition, and the current status of minority students and faculty in graduate psychology training programs. The last section reviews economic conditions, including median family income levels and poverty levels. However, before proceeding to specific demographic data, it is important that an overview of the U.S. Bureau of the Census's procedures for demographic counts be provided.

THE U.S. CENSUS AND ACCURATE DATA?

Much of the data for this chapter stems from the last decennial U.S. Census, conducted in 1980, and from the Census's Current Population Report surveys, conducted from 1980 to 1988, and summarized in the United States Bureau of the Census's (1989) *Statistical Abstract of the United States: 1988*. Additional data on educational achievement levels was summarized from the American Council on Education's (1988) Seventh Annual Status Report, and from Ponterotto's (in press b, in press c) recent affirmative action summary reports.

Counting every person in the United States with exact accuracy is an impossible task. Considering the enormity of this endeavor, the U.S. Bureau of the Census does a fairly good job of estimating population estimates disaggregated by gender, racial/ethnic group, age category, income levels, and so on. However, as noted by a number of multicultural authors, there are a number of limitations that must be considered when examining census data (see Casas, 1984; Markides & Mindel, 1987).

One limitation of the Census procedure regards data collection disaggregated by racial/ethnic group. More information, including recency of information, is available for select groups, namely Whites, Blacks, and Hispanics (particularly Mexican Americans and Puerto Ricans). Less comprehensive and recent information is available on Asian/Pacific Islanders and on Native Americans. The data presented throughout this chapter in both text and tabular form reflects this racial/ethnic group inconsistency.

Another concern with census data is the underreporting of population figures for racial/ethnic minority groups. Some minority politicians have noted that minorities are five to six times more likely than Whites not to be counted in census estimates. A number of reasons help explain this possibility. First, lower-income groups (in which racial/ethnic minorities are disproportionately represented) may be less reliable in completing census questionnaires because they are either skeptical of government-sponsored "paper-work," or they may have more trouble understanding and interpreting the questionnaires. Second, in the case of illegal immigrants, these individuals are hesitant, naturally, to complete any survey questionnaire that they think might identify them.

To examine a specific example of census underreporting, we turn to the 1980 decennial figures. In 1980, the census reported 14.6 million Hispanics in the United States. In examining this estimate, Ponterotto (1987) notes that the aggregate figured included an estimated 1.3 million illegal residents—probably a gross underestimate. Citing various statistical summary reports, Ponterotto (1987) estimated the 1980 Hispanic population to be closer to 20 million.

Another example of underreporting, or misreporting, can be seen in the case of the Native American population. Taking a rather thought provoking position, Forbes (1988) contends that the statistics on Native Americans may grossly underestimate the real number of Native Americans living in the United States. His position is based on the fact that the federal Office of Management and Budget definition of "American Indian" or "Alaska Native" includes persons having origins in *any* of the original peoples of *North America;* and yet persons of American indigenous race and culture who immigrate from Mexico and other Central and South American countries are automatically assigned to the "Hispanic" census category without having any opportunity to identify themselves also by their American Indian language and identity.

The U.S. Bureau of the Census is aware of the challenge to accurate racial/ethnic group reporting, and since 1980 they have made continual improvements in their data gathering methodology (see U.S. Bureau of the Census, 1988, "The Hispanic Population in the United States: March, 1985." Current Population Reports, Population Characteristics, Series P-20, No. 422). It is expected that when the 1990 decennial statistics become available, sometime in 1992, we will have a much better picture of America's "demographic face." With the various census reporting limitations now highlighted, attention is directed to the examination of relevant population figures.

POPULATION DEMOGRAPHICS

Table I presents 1980 U.S. Census population figures disaggregated by racial/ethnic group. From this table we note that racial/ethnic minorities, as a collective group, represented close to 20 percent of the total U.S. population in 1980. Blacks, the largest minority group, represented 11.3 percent of the population, followed by Hispanics with a representation rate of 6.2 percent.

Table I.
Population Figures by Racial Ethnic Group, 1980

Group	Totals (Millions)	Percentage Total
White	188.3	80.4
Black	26.5	11.3
American Indian, Eskimo, & Aleut	1.4	0.6
Asian/Pacific Islander	3.5	1.5
Hispanic	14.6	6.2
Total Minority Population	46.0	19.6
Total Population	234.4	100.0

Source: U.S. Bureau of the Census (1980). *Population Profile of the United States: 1980.* Population characteristics (Series P-25, No. 952). Washington, D.C.: U.S. Government Printing Office.

More recent and projected population figures, stemming from the Current Population Reports (U.S. Bureau of the Census, 1989), are available on Blacks, Whites, and Hispanics. Table II summarizes this information over the time periods 1989, 1990, 2000, and 2010. Looking across the four time periods it is apparent that the White population will witness marginal overall growth, while the Black and Hispanic populations will grow at an accelerated rate. For instance, during the ten-year period 1980–1990, the Hispanic population will grow 34.5 percent; the Black population, 15.8 percent; and the White cohort only 7.7 percent. By the year 2010, Whites will represent 76.7 percent of the total population, down from 80.7 percent in 1989; Blacks will represent 13.0 percent of the population, up from 11.8 percent in 1989; and Hispanics will represent 10.3 percent of the total U.S. population, up from 7.5 percent in 1989.

Table II.
Population Projections by Racial Ethnic Group: 1989 to 2010

Year	Racial/Ethnic Group			
	White	Black	Hispanic	Three Group Total
1989				
Population (1,000)	209,178	30,719	19,358	259,255
Percent of Total Popul.	80.7	11.8	7.5	100
1990				
Population (1,000)	210,616	31,148	19,887	261,651
Percent of Total Popul.	80.5	11.9	7.6	100
2000				
Population (1,000)	221,514	35,129	25,223	281,866
Percent of Total Popul.	78.6	12.5	8.9	100
2010				
Population (1,000)	228,978	38,833	30,795	298,606
Percent of Total Popul.	76.7	13.0	10.3	100
Percent Changes				
1980–1990	7.7	15.8	34.5	
1990–2000	5.2	12.8	26.8	
2000–2010	3.4	10.6	22.1	

Source: U.S. Bureau of the Census (1989). *Statistical Abstract of the United States: 1988* (109th edition). Washington, D.C.: 1989: Table 16, "Projections of the Hispanic Population by Age and Sex: 1988 to 2010"; Table 17, "Projections of the Total Population by Age, Sex, and Race: 1988 to 2010."

Demographic Age Breakdown

To gather an accurate understanding of diverse racial/ethnic groups in the United States, it is necessary to have a sense of their representation among various age-cohort groups. Such an understanding will enlighten educators and mental health professionals as to future learning and counseling needs of a maturing population.

The most up-to-date age-related racial/ethnic group data stems from

1987 and is summarized in the recent *Statistical Abstract of the United States* (U.S. Bureau of the Census, 1989). Table III summarizes this data across five distinct age-cohort groups. The relative youth of the racial/ethnic minority populations relative to Whites is evident in Table III. Looking at the Percent Distribution columns, we see that Whites are the most highly represented group in the 45–65 year old cohort (19.3%) and the 65 years and over group (12.4%). Whites are followed by Blacks and then Hispanics in terms of "older group" representation.

Table III.
Population by Age, Across White, Black, and Hispanic Populations, 1987

Racial/Ethnic Group	Under 5 Years	5–14 Years	15–44 Years	45–65 Years	65 Years & Over	Total Persons
			Age Categories			
Total Population						
Number (1,000)	18,130	33,972	113,811	44,901	27,975	238,789
Percent	7.6	14.2	47.7	18.8	11.7	100.0
White						
Number (1,000)	14,798	27,441	95,892	39,149	25,173	202,453
Percent	7.3	13.6	47.4	19.3	12.4	100.0
Black						
Number (1,000)	2,728	5,283	14,087	4,501	2,331	28,930
Percent	9.4	18.3	48.7	15.6	8.1	100.0
Total Hispanic						
Number (1,000)	1,995	3,691	9,705	2,493	906	18,790
Percent	10.6	19.6	51.6	13.3	4.8	100.0
Mexican						
Number (1,000)	1,341	2,553	6,006	1,373	491	11,762
Percent	11.4	21.7	51.1	11.7	4.2	100.0
Puerto Rican						
Number (1,000)	268	482	1,175	280	81	2,284
Percent	11.7	21.1	51.4	12.3	3.5	100.0

Source: U.S. Bureau of the Census (1989). *Statistical Abstract of the United States: 1988* (109th edition). Washington, D.C., 1989.

Table III reveals that in the 15–44 year-old cohort, Hispanics have the highest relative percentage, at 51.6 percent, followed by Blacks (48.7%) and Whites (47.4%). Hispanics are the highest represented group among the two youngest age-cohort groups. 10.6 percent of Hispanics are under five years of age, while only 9.4 percent of Blacks and 7.3 percent of Whites fall in this category. In the 5–14 year-old category, Hispanics have the highest relative percentage at 19.6 percent, followed by Blacks (18.3%) and Whites (13.6%).

Unfortunately, recent age-related data on Asian and Pacific Islanders, and Native Americans are not available. Thus to gather a global picture of age-related information relative to our five racial/ethnic groups of interest, we must look to original 1980 diecennial census data. Table IV presents the median ages across the five groups, as well as age-cohort specific information.

Table IV.
Age Categories for Major Racial Ethnic Groups: 1980

			Racial/Ethnic Group		
	White	Black	Hispanic	Asian/Pacific	Native Amer.
Median Age	31.3	24.9	23.2	28.6	23.0
Percentage Under 15 yrs. of age	21.3	28.7	32.0	25.0	31.8
Percentage Under 25 yrs. of age	39.5	50.3	53.9	42.3	54.3
Percentage Over 65 yrs. of age	12.2	7.9	7.9	6.1	5.3

Source: U.S. Bureau of the Census (1980). *Population Profile of the United States: 1980.* Population Characteristics (Series P-20, No. 363). (Washington, D.C.: U.S. Government Printing Office, 1980.)

In terms of median age, Native Americans (i.e., American Indians, Eskimos, and Aleuts) are the youngest, with a median age of 23.0, followed closely by Hispanics at 23.2 years. Looking across age-cohort categories, it is interesting to note that over 50 percent of Blacks, Hispanics, and Native Americans are under the age of 25 years.

Fertility Rates

An important indicator of growth patterns is the fertility rate among American females. According to Hodgkinson (1985), a leading populations demographer, in order to maintain its numerical representation in U.S. society, a particular racial/ethnic group must possess a fertility rate of 2.1 children per female. Currently, the fertility rate for White females is 1.7; for Puerto Ricans, 2.1, for Mexican Americans, 2.9, and for Blacks, 2.4. These figures, coupled with the fact that more and more Black and Hispanic women are entering the child-bearing years of their lives, while more and more White women are leaving them (see Tables III and IV again), explain in part the projected high growth rate for many racial/ethnic minority populations (Ponterotto, in press c).

The combined youthfulness and growth of the racial/ethnic minority population is already quite evident in our nation's elementary schools. Citing the work of Hodgkinson (1985), Ponterotto (in press a) notes the following statistics: as of 1985, over 50 percent of California's elementary school population was racial/ethnic minority; 46 percent of Texas school children are minority; and all of the country's 25 largest city school systems have "minority majorities." Further, it is estimated that by the year 2000, 33 percent of all elementary school children will be minority, and by the year 2020, this percentage will rise to 39 percent (One-Third of A Nation, 1988; Ponterotto, in press a). At this point, it is important to examine in more detail the current status of racial/ethnic minorities in our educational system.

EDUCATIONAL DATA SUMMARY

Familiarity with educational statistics and trends is important because educational achievement is closely linked to economic status, which in turn predicates lifestyle and environmental comfort (see Gibbs & Huang, 1989a). This section reviews various educational achievement trends among our racial/ethnic groups of interest. Specific educational achievement indices examined include high school and college completion rates, general higher education representation, drop-out statistics, and minority representation in the field of psychology.

High School and College Completion Rates

According to the most recent supplementary reports of the U.S. Census (U.S. Bureau of the Census, 1989 [Table 44] reporting 1987 data), 76.9 percent of Whites, 63.5 percent of Blacks, 53.9 percent of Puerto Ricans, and 44.8 percent of Mexican Americans 25 years of age or older completed four years of high school or more. On the college level, 20.5 percent of Whites, 10.7 percent of Blacks, 8.0 percent of Puerto Ricans, and 5.8 percent of Mexican Americans completed four or more years of college.

Recent national data on high school and college completion rates are not available on Asian Americans, Pacific Islanders, and Native Americans. However, 1980 Census data (as reported in U.S. Bureau of the Census,

1989, Table 45) notes that 75.3 percent of Asians (including but not limited to Chinese, Filipino, Japanese, Asian Indian, Korean, and Vietnamese) 25 years of age or older completed 4 years of high school or more. Parallel figures for Pacific Islanders (including, but not limited to Hawaiians, Guamanians, and Samoans) were 67.2 percent, and for Native Americans (including American Indians, Eskimos, and Aleuts), 55.5 percent.

With respect to college figures, 34.3 percent of Asians, 9.3 percent of Pacific Islanders, and 7.7 percent of Native Americans 25 years of age and older have completed four or more years of college (1980 census data reported in U.S. Bureau of the Census, 1989, Table 45).

Higher Education Enrollments

Table V summarizes the most recent data available for student enrollments in higher education (from American Council on Education, 1988; Ponterotto, in press c), and for faculty and administration representation on campus (American Council on Education, 1988; Ponterotto, in press b). To place this data in perspective, the last row of Table V presents the overall societal representation of the major racial/ethnic groups.

Among the more salient findings evident in Table V are the figures related to general minority representation among various university cohorts. Total minority representation according to 1980 Census figures is 19.6 percent (and this is most likely a highly underrepresented figure for 1990); and from column 6 of Table V, it is clear then that racial/ethnic minorities are underrepresented at each level of university participation. Particularly noteworthy is that racial/ethnic minorities represent only 10 percent of the full-time faculty (and many of these faculty are at the lower ends of the academic ladder [see Ponterotto, in press b]).

Looking at racial/ethnic group-specific data, we note the following trends. In relation to their societal representation (80.4%), Whites are overrepresented among faculty (90.0%), administrators (88.4%), and professional students (85.2%). Whites are slightly underrepresented as undergraduates (79.2%), graduate students (78.9%), and in the total student body (79.3%).

Blacks are underrepresented at every level of higher education. Particularly noteworthy is the fact that although Blacks represent 11.3 percent of the total U.S. population, they represent only 4.1% of the university faculty, 5.0 percent of graduate students, and 5.2 percent of professional students.

Table V.
Racial/Ethnic Group Representation in Higher Education:
Students, Administrators, and Faculty, 1985 or 1986
(Percentage of Total)

	White	Black	Hispanics	Asian/ Pacific	American Indian	Total Minority	International Students
Undergraduates (1986)	79.2	9.2	5.3	3.6	0.8	18.9	1.9
Graduate Students (1986)	78.9	5.0	3.2	3.0	0.4	11.6	9.5
Professional Students (1986)	85.2	5.2	3.4	4.2	0.4	13.2	1.5
Total (all students) (1986)	79.3	8.6	5.0	3.6	0.7	17.9	2.8
Full-Time Adminis. (1985)	88.4	7.6	2.0	1.5	0.4	11.5	
Full-Time Faculty (1985)	90.0	4.1	1.7	3.9	0.3	10.0	
Societal Representation, 1980	80.4	11.3	6.2	1.5	0.6	19.6	

Source: American Council on Education (1988). *Minorities in Higher Education.* Seventh Annual Status Report, Office of Minority Concerns, Washington, D.C.: Tables 5, 7, 8, 11, and 14; Ponterotto, 1990b, 1990c.

Hispanics, as well, are underrepresented at every level of campus life. Representing 6.2 percent of the U.S. population (this is probably a gross underestimate, see Ponterotto [1987]), they represent only 1.7 percent of the higher education faculty, 2.0 percent of administrators, and 5.0 percent of the total student body.

Asian Americans are very well represented in higher education, as evidenced in their overrepresentation among all university cohort groups with the exception of full-time administrators, where their 1.5 percent representation equals their overall societal representation. Finally, relative to their societal representation (0.6%) [a gross underestimate as previously explained; see Forbes, 1988], American Indians seem adequately represented as college undergraduates (0.8%), but underrepresented as graduate and professional students (0.4%), faculty (0.3%), and administrators (0.4%).

In examining Table V it is important to note that the societal representation date (last row) came from 1980 U.S. Census figures, which probably represents a gross underestimate relative to the 1985 and 1986 figures used for the specific university cohort groups. The 1985/1986 racial/ethnic minority representation in society is most likely higher for the minority groups (particularly Hispanics), and lower for the White majority than is portrayed in the last row of Table V.

Racial/Ethnic Group Enrollments by Type of Institution

Table VI presents a microscopic breakdown of student higher education enrollments for 1986, the most recently available at this writing. Table VI indicates that for all racial/ethnic groups, with the exception of Asians, women represent the majority on campus (see row 1). Row 2 of Table VI reveals that American Indians (12.2%) and Hispanics (13.5%) have the lowest representation in private institutions, and Whites the highest (22.8%).

Table VI.
Enrollment by Racial/Ethnic Group, Gender and Type Institution
in Numbers (1,000) and Percentages

Category					Racial Ethnic Group					
	Amer. Ind.		Asian		Black		Hispanic		White	
	No.	%	No.	%	No.	%	No.	%	No.	%
Men	40	44.7	239	53.3	436	40.3	292	46.8	4646	46.9
Women	51	56.7	209	46.7	645	59.7	332	53.2	5268	53.1
Public	79	87.8	372	83.0	855	79.1	539	86.4	7650	77.2
Private	11	12.2	76	17.0	226	20.9	84	13.5	2264	22.8
Four-Year	40	44.4	262	58.5	615	56.9	278	44.6	6340	63.9
Two-Year	51	56.7	186	41.5	466	43.1	345	55.3	3575	36.1
Undergraduate	84	93.3	394	87.9	995	92.0	569	91.2	8552	86.3
Graduate	5	5.6	43	9.6	72	6.7	46	7.4	1132	11.4
Professional	1	1.1	11	2.5	14	1.3	9	1.4	230	2.3
Total	90		448		1081		624		9914	

Note: Information synthesized from Chronicle of Higher Education, July 6, 1988; and Ponterotto, 1990c. Data is from the Department of Education Survey, 1986. Percentages may not add up to 100 due to rounding.

With regards to comparative enrollments in two- and four-year colleges, American Indians and Hispanics are the only groups with greater representation among two-year colleges. The implications of this data are particularly noteworthy because the educational pipeline from two to four year colleges has not been very successful for minorities (Richardson & Bender, 1987). A majority of minority students enrolled in two-year institutions never do go on to collect their bacca-laureate degrees.

Finally, in the last row of Table VI we note that Whites and Asians have the highest proportionate representation in graduate and profes-sional schools, whereas American Indians, Blacks, and Hispanics are mostly represented at the undergraduate level.

Racial/Ethnic Minority Student Attrition in Higher Education

It is clear that students from some racial/ethnic subgroups are more likely to leave college prematurely (Ponterotto, in press c). Recent data suggests that of the 1980 high school graduates who entered postsecondary education, 42 percent of Puerto Ricans, 31 percent of Blacks, 28 percent of Mexican Americans, and 26 percent of Whites left school by February of 1984 (Wilson & Justiz, 1987/1988).

According to the American Council on Education (1988), of the 1980 high school graduates who enrolled in higher education by 1982, 71 percent of Blacks, 66 percent of Hispanics, 65 percent of American Indians, 55 percent of Whites, and 47 percent of Asians left college by 1986 without their completed degrees (see Ponterotto, in press c for an extensive discussion of minority students in higher education).

Racial/Ethnic Minority Representation in Psychology Programs

Virtually all scholars in the multicultural area acknowledge that the profession of psychology needs more members of racial/ethnic minority groups amongst its ranks (Atkinson et al., 1989; Katz, 1985; Parker, 1988; Ponterotto & Casas, 1987; D.W. Sue, 1981; D. W. Sue & D. Sue, in press). Racial/ethnic minority psychologists serve as influential successful role models for their constituents, and many of them have a high degree of familiarity and experience with minority populations. It is therefore most appropriate to examine the status of racial/ethnic minority stu-dents and faculty in graduate psychology departments.

Table VII presents the most recent enrollment figures available (1987–1988) at this writing for racial/ethnic group student representation in master degree programs, doctoral programs, and among department of psychology faculty. The data reveals that racial/ethnic minorities are better represented as doctoral students in psychology (11.28%) than as masters degree students (9.69%) or faculty (5.38%). According to Table VII,

Blacks are the minority group most represented as graduate students and faculty in psychology, and American Indians the least represented. Representation figures for the other racial/ethnic groups are evident in Table VII.

Table VII.
Racial/Ethnic Group Representation (Percentage)
Among Graduate Psychology Students and Faculty, 1987-1988

	White	Black	Hispanic	Asian Pacific	American Indian	Total Minority	Not Specified	Total
Full-Time Doctoral Students								
Numbers	15,115	705	622	611	67	2005	625	17,745
Percent	85.2	4.0	3.5	3.4	0.4	11.3	3.5	100
Full-Time Master Degree Students								
Numbers	6,339	292	266	191	31	780	929	8,048
Percent	78.8	3.6	3.3	2.4	0.4	9.7	11.5	100
Full-Time Faculty								
Numbers	6,459	184	86	82	12	364	30	6,853
Percent	94.3	2.7	1.3	1.2	0.2	5.4	0.4	100

Source: "Sex, Race/Ethnicity Data in Survey . . ." *Chronicle of Higher Education*, 1988, Vol. 19, No. 11, p. 40. Totals and percentages adjusted for missing data.

With regards to the field of Counseling Psychology specifically, recent surveys conducted by the Council for Counseling Psychology Training Programs report that although programs are attracting more students overall to the field in recent years, the number of new racial/ethnic minority students has remained stagnant (see Cameron, Galassi, Birk, & Waggener, 1989; Gallessich & Olmstead, 1987; Richardson & Massey, 1986).

ECONOMIC CONDITIONS

Table VIII summarizes family income information disaggregated by racial/ethnic group for the most recent data available — 1987 (reported in U.S. Bureau of the Census, 1989). Some of the more salient information highlighted in Table VIII includes the following. Whites are clearly more highly represented at the three highest income levels. Interestingly, the White population has its highest within-group representation (22.0%) in the $50,000 and over income bracket. By comparison, Blacks and Mexican Americans have their highest within-group representation in the $15,000 to $25,000 income bracket, at 20.2 percent and 24.1 percent respectively. Puerto Ricans are most represented (19.6%) in the $5,000 to $10,000 income bracket.

Analyzing the data in a more aggregate fashion, we note that in the three highest income brackets combined ($25,000 and over) are found 61.2 percent of White families, 35.9 percent of Black families, 37.0 percent of Mexican families, and 30.3 percent of Puerto Rican families (this combined data is not shown separately in Table VIII).

Data related to median income levels and total persons below the poverty level, are represented in Table VIII as well. Whites have the highest median income level of the four racial/ethnic groups appearing in Table VIII, at $30,809; and Puerto Ricans have the lowest median income, at $14,584. Not surprisingly then, Whites also have the fewest percentage below the poverty level, 11.0 percent; and Puerto Ricans have the highest relative representation in poverty, at 39.4 percent.

Economic information of relevance to our discussion, but not included in Table VIII regards residence ownership. According to the latest available national census data (U.S. Bureau of the Census, 1989), in 1987 66.8 percent of Whites, 45.4 percent of Blacks, and 40.6 percent of Hispanics owned their places of residence. By contrast, 31.4 percent of Whites, 52.9 percent of Blacks, and 57.2 percent of Hispanics rent their primary living quarters.

The above information has focused on Whites, Blacks, and Hispanics because very recent national census data is only available on these groups. For accurate national data on Asian Americans and American Indian groups, we must again turn to the 1980 U.S. census (as summarized in U.S. Bureau of the Census, 1989, Table 45). The median family income (in 1979 dollars) for the aggregate Asian group was $23,095. It is important to note that there is quite a bit of variability in income levels between various Asian American subgroups. For instance, Japanese Americans had a median income of $27,354 (remember this is 1979 dollars), whereas Vietnamese had a median family income of only $12,840.

Among Pacific Island groups, the aggregate median income of $17,984 in 1979 dollars could be further disaggregated by specific island group, as follows: Hawaiians, $19,196, Guamanians, $18,218, and Samoan, $12,242. The Native American median family income in 1979 dollars was $13,724.

Table VIII.

Family Income of White, Black, and Hispanic Populations, 1987

	Number (1,000)			Hispanicᵇ			Percent Distribution			Hispanicᵇ		
	Total Popl.ᵃ	White	Black	Totalᶜ	Mexican	Puerto Rican	Total Popl.ᵃ	White	Black	Totalᶜ	Mexican	Puerto Rican
Total Families	64,491	55,696	7,096	4,403	2,611	593	100	100	100	100	100	100
Less than												
$ 5,000	3,008	1,947	994	381	208	105	4.7	3.5	14.0	8.7	8.0	17.7
$ 5,000–$ 9,999	5,022	3,747	1,146	643	365	116	7.8	6.7	16.1	14.6	14.0	19.6
$10,000–$14,999	6,232	5,047	977	668	441	81	9.7	9.1	13.8	15.2	16.9	13.7
$15,000–$24,999	12,613	10,875	1,435	985	629	110	19.6	19.5	20.2	22.4	24.1	18.5
$25,000–$34,999	11,654	10,332	1,053	727	432	80	18.1	18.6	14.7	16.5	16.5	13.5
$35,000–$49,999	12,632	11,461	878	550	323	56	19.6	20.6	12.4	12.5	12.4	9.4
$50,000 or more	13,328	12,267	624	450	212	44	20.7	22.0	8.8	10.2	8.1	7.4
Median Income $	29,458	30,809	16,604	19,995	19,326	14,584						
Persons Below Poverty Level	32,370	22,188	8,983	5,117	3,333	898	13.6	11.0	31.1	27.3	28.4	39.4

ᵃIncludes other races and persons not of Hispanic origin, not shown separately.
ᵇHispanic persons may be of any race.
ᶜIncludes other Hispanic subgroups not shown separately.
Source: United States Bureau of the Census (1989). *Statistical abstract of the United States: 1988* (109th edition). Washington, D.C., 1989.

The majority of this group is represented by American Indians, with a median family income level of $13,678.

Finally, according to the 1980 census, 10.3 percent of Asian families, 16.1 percent of Pacific Island families, and 23.7 percent of Native American families had income levels falling below the poverty level (U.S. Bureau of the Census, 1989, Table 45).

CONCLUSION

This chapter has summarized basic demographic information on various racial/ethnic groups. It goes without saying that counselors have a professional and ethical responsibility to keep abreast of demographic changes as they affect one's clinical practice and subject research pools.

Aggregate data presented in this chapter indicate that racial/ethnic minorities are becoming a more significant proportion of the total U.S. population. In terms of educational and socioeconomic success, the data indicate that, generally, Native Americans, Black Americans, and Hispanic Americans lag far behind that of Whites and *some* Asian American subgroups. Naturally, lower educational achievement and economic gain predicate increased life stressors and greater mental health service needs (see Gibbs & Huang, 1989a). *Given these statistics there should be no doubt that multicultural issues are becoming increasingly central to the mission of the counseling and mental health professions.*

Chapter Four

RACIAL/ETHNIC MINORITY COUNSELING PRACTICE AND RESEARCH: HISTORICAL PERSPECTIVES

T o appreciate the existing need for a book that addresses racial/ethnic minority research and issues comprehensively and with depth, it is important to place the book within a historical perspective vis-a-vis the profession. To this end, this chapter provides a historical overview of the profession's slow but evolving efforts to recognize, understand, and effectively deal with the service, training and research needs of racial/ ethnic minorities.

HISTORICAL OVERVIEW

The importance of considering sociocultural characteristics was brought to the fore as early as 1962 by C. Gilbert Wrenn who warned of the dangers of becoming culturally encapsulated, that is, viewing and interpreting the experiences of a culturally-different client from one's own ethnocentric and monocultural viewpoint (i.e, a White middle-class viewpoint). More specifically, he cautioned against the imposition of culturally-alien goals, values, and practices upon counselees from diverse cultural backgrounds. From a more active perspective, Kenneth Clark (1971) put forth the challenge of determining ways in which social responsibility can be integrated as a dominant theme of the science and profession of psychology. Seven years later, APA President Brewster Smith called for a systematic assessment of the status of minorities within the profession.

In the twenty-eight-year period since the initial Wrenn statement, a number of professional efforts have been directed towards developing the organizational mechanisms to sensitize and prepare the counseling profession to effectively work with our increasing multicultural society. The material presented in this chapter briefly and nonexhaustively summarizes those efforts that have been most instrumental in guiding the counseling profession towards this end. For further details relative to these efforts, the reader is referred to Casas (1984) and to Comas-Diaz (in press), the sources from which much of the following material has been abstracted and summarized.

1963 — The Ad Hoc Committee on Equal Opportunity in Psychology was charged with exploring the possible problems with training and employment in psychology as a consequence of race. More specifically, this charge translated into two major objectives: (1) to explore the question of equality of opportunity in employment of Black Psychologists in professional and academic positions; and (2) to examine the recruitment and selection of students for training in psychology.

1967 — The Ad hoc committee described above was made a standing committee and charged with the formulation of policy related to the education, training, employment, and status of minority groups in psychology. During the period between 1971 and 1974, the concerns of this committee grew to include the status of women and other issues of sexism, advocacy for victims of racism, instigation of affirmative action under HEW regulations, APA internships programs at Central Office, the Visiting Scientists Program, and Project Impact (the forerunner of the Minority Fellowship Program).

Being charged with such diverse programs and responsibilities, in 1974 the committee requested clarification of its structure, function, and responsibility. Subsequently, action was taken to reduce ambiguity by more specifically charging the committee to address specific issues and concerns relative to the four major racial/ethnic groups (i.e., Asian Americans, Blacks, Hispanics, and Native Americans).

1969 — The Commission on Accelerating Black Participation in Psychology was established to serve as an intermediate step in APA's response to the challenge of action with regard to the needs of Black Americans. More specifically, it was charged to direct its efforts towards dealing with any barriers that Blacks might encounter relative to funding sources, avenues of communication, and access to leadership.

1970 — APA established the Office of the Black Students' Psychological Association to address the needs of Black students. The efforts of this association resulted in a program that included guidelines for the following: (a) recruitment of Black students and faculty members into psychology; (b) gathering and dissemination of financial aid information for Black students; (c) design of programs offering meaningful community experience for Black students in psychology; and (d) development of terminal programs at all degree levels that would equip Black students with the tools necessary to function within the Black community (Korman, 1974). These guidelines were to set the tone for future requests put forth by other racial/ethnic minority groups to APA.

1971 — In response to the challenge put forth by Kenneth Clark (1971), the Board of Social and Ethical Responsibility in Psychology (BSERP) was created to oversee three committees — the Committee on Academic Freedom and Conditions of Employment, the Committee on Women, and the Committee on Equal Opportunity in Psychology, as well as a myriad of task forces dealing with such issues as ethics in testing and the moral implications of the Vietnam War.

1973 — While APA was slowly attempting to address racial/ethnic minority needs, growing concerns and criticism by a substantial number of psychologists eventuated in a call for a National Conference on Levels and Patterns of Professional Training in Psychology (Korman, 1974). The call for such a conference induced NIMH to provide resources supporting the Vail Conference which was held in 1973. This Conference began the process of dealing with the central issue of ethnic minority entry into professional psychology. Since the issue of professional training for ethnic minorities had been almost totally ignored by previous training conferences, it is significant that the concerns of ethnic minorities achieved such prominence at Vail. In fact, a Task Group on Professional Training and Minority Groups was included in the conference (Korman, 1974).

In retrospect, this is not surprising given the fact that Vail was the first national conference to actively seek representation on its steering committee from previously disenfranchised groups. The presence of representatives of minorities on this committee was eventually reflected in all aspects of the conference: format, content, and selection of participants. While the exclusion of racial/ethnic minority participants from each conference from Boulder in 1949 to Chicago in 1965 had resulted in the absence of any recommendations geared specifically to the needs of minorities, such was not the case at Vail.

Though specifically directed at clinical psychology, the recommendations that resulted from the Vail Conference had a direct impact on counseling psychology as well. More specifically, the conference's concern with the implementation of affirmative action programs and the identification, recruitment, admission, and graduation of minority students was viewed as a basic ethical obligation.

In addition, the participants felt that it was important for all students to be prepared to function professionally in a pluralistic society. To this end, it was suggested that: (a) training experience should occur in a multicultural context both within the university and in the fieldwork settings; (b) the content of training must adequately prepare students for their eventual professional roles vis-a-vis a wide diversity of target groups; and (c) students must be helped to maintain a balance between acculturation into professional and scholarly roles and retention of their group's identity and cultural sensitivity to the identity of other groups.

Due to a general dissatisfaction with the scope of APA's response to the concerns of ethnic minorities, the conference participants subsequently proposed and accepted resolutions that were more structural in nature and which recommended the following: (a) that a Board of Minority Advocacy, composed of representatives of ethnic minority groups be created in APA and be responsible for examining policies regarding minority concerns; (b) that this Board have prior review functions regarding other organizational units of APA and that it advise the Board of Directors in the general area of ethnic minority affairs; and (c) that an Office of Minority Affairs be created, with responsibility for monitoring and evaluating APA projects, programs, and policies, for developing and disseminating information related to minority concerns, and for initiating appropriate relationships with public and private agencies.

1974—The APA Minority Fellowship Program (funded by NIMH) was initiated in 1974. This program sought to increase the representation of ethnic minorities in psychology by providing stipends to students and by helping psychology departments to develop cultural diversity. According to S. Sue (1981):

> ...the impact of the Program was significant. Recruitment, educational opportunities, and support of ethnic minority students were increased. In many departments, the Program's efforts affected the recruitment of ethnic minority faculty, curriculum, and the education not only of ethnic students but of *all* students (p. 23).

1978—By this time, it was well acknowledged within APA that the Committee on Equality of Opportunity in Psychology and the Board of Social and Ethical Responsibility in Psychology had primary responsibilities for issues relevant to racial/ethnic minority groups. However, it was also noted that the focus of these two bodies had broadened from specific issues of race (especially Blacks) to include all minorities, as well as a myriad of other issues of importance but not directly concerned with minority affairs.

Consequently, racial/ethnic minority professionals expressed the concern that broadening the focus of these bodies had impeded the expected progress of racial/ethnic minorities within APA. This concern eventually served as a major impetus for the Dulles Conference of 1978 that examined, from an action-oriented perspective, means of expanding the roles of culturally diverse people in psychology.

S. Sue (1981) contends that this event (funded by APA and NIMH) was momentous for the following reasons:

> First, it marked the first time that many persons of diverse ethnic backgrounds (American Indians, Asian Americans, Blacks, and Hispanic Americans) convened with APA officers and administrators to discuss issues of concern and to develop recommendations for the pluralism of psychology. Second, the conference allowed relationships to be tested: Ethnic minority psychologists versus APA; one ethnic group versus another; and members of one group versus other members of the same group. Similar to the situation at political conventions, different factions were concerned that their own interests receive full attention. Third, the conflict between caucuses and factions, while intense and potentially disruptive, actually served to unify Conference participants. Greater awareness emerged of the issues confronting each group and of the need to accommodate different interests and value systems. Indeed consensus was achieved over the necessity to go beyond the interests of one group and to fully respect other groups and the concept of diversity (p. 23–24).

The result of such inter- and intra-group discussions was unanimous support for the conclusion that there was a need for a clearer focus on minority affairs at APA and, more importantly, for the recommendations that such a focus could best be attained through establishment of a Board of Minority Affairs, a Minority Affairs Office, and eventually a racial/ethnic minority division.

1979—Thus, the Board of Directors, and subsequently, the Council of Representatives, took action establishing the Minority Affairs Office and creating an Ad Hoc Committee on Minority Affairs. The major responsibilities of these two bodies were to conduct research and prepare a report specifying the major structural and conceptual issues of concern to racial/ethnic minority psychologists and to present a succinct set of recommendations to address these concerns. Two areas of concern highlighted in the eventual report included: (a) effective minority representation within the APA governance system; and (b) the development of a broadly-based psychology incorporating contributions from ethnic minority perspectives with existing psychological knowledge.

1981—With respect to minority representation in the APA governance system, a recommendation was again made that a board of ethnic minority affairs be created, and after extensive educational and lobbying efforts among APA members, such a board was finally created in 1981. The establishment of this board is significant because it institutionalized within APA governance structure a mechanisms to enhance the pluralism of psychology.

The Board, composed of eleven members, is concerned with those aspects of psychology which impact ethnic minorities. Major responsibilities of the Board of Ethnic Minority Affairs (BEMA) include: (a) increasing scientific understanding of those aspects of psychology that pertain to culture and ethnicity; (b) increasing the quality and quantity of educational and training opportunities for ethnic minority persons in psychology, and (c) promoting the development of culturally-sensitive models for the delivery of psychological services.

As indicated in BEMA's charge, two of its highest priorities were minority education and training issues. For instance, the BEMA Subcommittee on Culturally-Sensitive Models conducted a nationwide survey to assess the specific types of culturally-relevant course material and experiences that were offered in the clinical training of graduate students. The survey results indicated a very marginal inclusion of culturally-sensitive material, mostly offered at the internship level rather than at the graduate level (Wyatt & Parham, 1985).

In spite of these findings, several programs requested information regarding the inclusion of culturally-sensitive materials. Thus, in 1981, responding to the educational training needs reflected in the survey, the Task Force on Minority Education and Training was established to address the recommendations on education and training that were accepted by the Board of Ethnic Minority Affairs.

The Task Force was specifically established to concentrate on issues relative to the training of psychologists who work with culturally-diverse populations, the underrepresentation of ethnic minority psychologists in the profession, and the funding of education and training opportunities for minorities in psychology. In addition, the Task Force worked on the development of psychology curriculum materials for ethnic minorities (see Comas-Diaz, in press).

1982—The Board of Ethnic Minority Affairs acknowledging the importance of the work that could be conducted by the Task Force, expanded its charge to include the development of a proposal for a Continuing Committee on Minority Education and Training (se Comas-Diaz, in press).

1985—The APA Council approved the Continuing Committee on Ethnic Minority Human Resources Development. Upon this approval, the Committee identified two major areas of concern: (a) recruitment and retention of ethnic minority students and faculty; and (b) development of ethnic minority education and training resources. The Committee began advocating training in cultural diversity as a prerequisite to providing psychological services to ethnic minority populations. In order to accomplish this, the Committee presented to the Association a position paper urging that multicultural awareness be added to the criteria used to define and prescribe the philosophy, goals, curricula, practica and composition of training in psychology just as scientific rigor and clinical expertise are currently used.

1985—Following through with the final recommendation put forth by the Dulles Conference, a separate division of APA, Division 45, was established to facilitate the full participation of racial/ethnic minority persons as well as persons interested in racial/ethnic minority issues and concerns in the total decision-making structure of APA.

1987—In June 1987, a National Conference on Graduate Education in Psychology was held at the University of Utah in Salt Lake City (see Bickman, 1987). The major focus of this Conference was to discuss issues and prepare recommendations for potential changes in graduate education. Acknowledging the fact that the recognition of differences among people, such as those that may be associated with age, sex, socioeconomic, and ethnic backgrounds is an important component of the Ethical Principles of Psychologists (APA, 1981), the Conference recognized cultural diversity as an important aspect of graduate education.

The Conference further acknowledged that "despite some impressive strides in the desirable direction, it is clear that insufficient attention has been devoted to the importance of cultural diversity to psychology as a discipline and as a profession" (APA, 1987, p. 1078). More specifically, the Conference concluded that "there is no doubt that in the past decade the number of graduate psychology courses focusing on cultural diversity has increased" (APA, 1987, p. 1079). There was less satisfaction expressed with respect to the way in which findings and insights about the influences of diversity have been included in psychology courses that are not focused solely on cultural differences. Nor was there widespread satisfaction with the extent to which issues of diversity are deliberately included in practicum training. To this end, graduate programs were encouraged to provide an emphasis in formal course and fieldwork that relates to cultural diversity.

More to the point of action, a resolution was passed directing APA to: (a) apprise all faculty of the desirability of including appropriate information relative to cultural diversity within their course outlines and teaching materials; (b) provide workshops for faculty/staff development to examine policy pertaining to barriers in communicating initial research on emerging topics; (c) publish special issues in journals; and (d) create a clearinghouse of scholars from minority and other underrepresented groups to visit graduate departments as consultants, speakers, visiting professors to inform/update faculty and students on issues of cultural diversity (APA, 1987).

AN APA DIVISIONAL PERSPECTIVE

While major organizational and policy efforts were being extended by APA as a whole, specific actions relative to racial/ethnic minority issues and concerns were being taken by individual divisions of APA. For instance, in Division 17, Counseling Psychology, the Education and Training Committee made recommendations with respect to service and training objectives for ethnic minorities over the coming decade (Myers, 1982). With respect to service, it was recommended that Counseling Psychology monitor the changing demographic situation in terms of shifting population bulges to determine the focus of needed services. It was also recommended that there be renewed commitment to the recruitment and retention of minority students to help serve the needs of this population. Focusing on education and training, the Division recommended that training programs pay greater attention to the increasing diversity of our society.

1982—Taking a stronger and more directive position relative to cross-cultural counseling, a position paper recommending the adoption of specific cross-cultural counseling and therapy competencies by the American Psychological Association to be used as accreditation criteria was published under the auspices of Division 17 (Sue, D., Bernier, Durran, Feinberg, Pedersen, Smith, & Vasquez-Nuttal, 1982). At present, steps are being taken to develop a well-defined plan of action that will facilitate the implementation of these competencies.

1987—The third in a series of national conference for counseling psychology was held in Atlanta, Georgia. With the title "Planning the Future," a major theme that ran throughout all of the Conference's invited work groups was the need to reaffirm Counseling Psychology's traditional awareness of "the importance of viewing people and their behavior . . . (within) . . . a sociocultural context influenced by variables of culture, ethnicity, gender, sexual orientation, age, and sociohistorical perspective" (Rude, Weissberg, & Gazda, 1988, p. 426).

One of the conference work groups (Gelso, Betz, Friedlander, Helms, Hill, Patton, Super, & Wampold, 1988) was charged with looking at the future directions of research within the field of counseling. Breaking new ground, this group put forth research recommendations that directly addressed racial/ethnic minority issues. The recommendations focused on (a) an increased quantity of racial/ethnic minority research using accurate terminology and focusing on theory development, testing, and application; (b) a need for studies examining actual interventions in the cross-cultural area; and (c) the incorporation of nontraditional or alternative research approaches (as we discuss in Chapter Nine).

1988—Division 17 moves to make its Ad Hoc Committee on Cultural Diversity and Ethnic/Gender Issues a standing committee. This Committee is charged with providing input to Division 17 on any service, training and/or research issues that impact racial/ethnic minorities.

EFFORTS OF THE AMERICAN ASSOCIATION FOR COUNSELING AND DEVELOPMENT

Complimenting and actually predating the accomplishments of APA relative to racial/ethnic minorities were actions taken by the American Association for Counseling and Development (AACD) previously called the American Personnel and Guidance Association (APGA).

1965—As early as this year, this Association established a Human Rights Commission supporting human dignity regardless of race, color, creed, sex, affectional or sexual orientation, age, and/or handicap.

1969—The National Office of Non-White Concerns was established to work with the governing bodies of AACD to determine and implement policies and positions relating to non-White groups. At the same time varied resolutions were passed by the Association calling for actions to insure that the service and professional needs of non-White groups were met. One such resolution directed AACD to take action to see that non-White persons be appointed to policy-making committees dealing with counselor education and supervision and the accreditation of counseling programs.

1972—The Association for Non-White Concerns, now called the Association for Multicultural Counseling and Development, was established as a division of AACD to directly represent the concerns of non-White members within AACD's governing structure.

1977—At the divisional level, the Association for Counselor Education and Supervision (ACES) adopted a position paper on Non-White Concerns that urged all persons involved in counseling to establish policies, procedures and activities which would improve services for non-White persons. It also called for the development of training programs which would encompass the unique needs and aspirations of non-Whites. Finally, it directed its officers and affiliates to support and conduct activities which would help to implement the positions contained in the papers (ACES Commission on Non-White Concerns, 1979).

RACIAL/ETHNIC MINORITIES: A HISTORICAL RESEARCH PERSPECTIVE

Paralleling the organizational efforts, varied individuals were also taking steps to make research more sensitive and responsive to racial/ethnic minority needs, concerns, and topics. This was especially true with respect to the last decade during which time:

> there has been increased theoretical and empirical attention given to cross-cultural issues in the phenomena that counseling psychologists study, for example, counseling. There has also been increased attention to research on minority groups of various kinds. Although noting this increase, however, it is important to keep in mind where we started. A decade ago, research on minorities (e.g., racial, ethnic, sexual preference, etc.) and on cross-cultural issues was virtually nonexistent. We have clearly increased our output, but much more work is needed.

> Although according to at least one observer (Whiteley, 1984), cross-cultural counseling and therapy had become a legitimate interest area by the early 1970s, scientific interest in the topic has been slow to develop. One suspects that the slow pace may be a consequence of the sociopolitical origins of the topic, that is, in the civil rights movement of the 1960s. As the concept of "cultural" became equivalent to "minority," and as the concept of minority

became all too frequently fixed on people of color or linguistic diversity, multicultural counseling research appears to have been compartmentalized into a separate category whose content is all too often seen as having little relevance to White people or those in the majority culture. It is crucial that the specialty as a whole and its individual membership self-consciously work at decompartmentalizing. Cross-cultural and minority group research must not be placed into an airtight compartment, carried on by a small group of scholars, and essentially ignored by the rest (Gelso et al., 1988, p. 395–396).

CONCLUSION

The psychological profession has come a long way in paying heed to Wrenn's (1962) warnings of the dangers of becoming culturally encapsulated. This has been especially true with respect to its efforts to develop the organizational mechanisms to sensitize and prepare the profession to effectively work with our increasing multicultural society. Though the desired attainments have not been as impressive as those reached along organizational lines, the profession has also taken strides to improve the representation of racial/ethnic minorities within its ranks. It has also begun to identify and develop the process by which the needs of racial/ethnic minorities are more adequately included and addressed in the curricula and training experiences required of all psychologists.

As one purveys the historical attainments of the profession via-a-vis racial/ethnic minorities that are documented in this chapter, it becomes blatantly evident that an area in which the profession has tended to encapsulate itself has been the area of research. This is truly unfortunate given the fact that as previously stated in this book, research is the cornerstone that supports all other relevant professional activities.

Although a variety of reasons could be given to explain the profession's propensity to ignore research in its efforts to address racial/ethnic minority concerns and issues, a major reason that merits serious considerations and one that is addressed in greater depth in Chapter Ten is the prevailing professional belief that research is comprised of professional behaviors that are value free, a-political, a-cultural, and overall humanistic in nature. Unfortunately, this belief is totally untrue; furthermore, adherence to it has much too frequently resulted in negative consequences to racial/ethnic minority communities as will be made evident in Chapter Five.

Chapter Five

VALUE SYSTEMS IN COUNSELING:
A RACIAL/ETHNIC MINORITY PERSPECTIVE

Values play an extremely important role in the counseling process. A counselor's value system affects his or her beliefs and attitudes which in turn influence his or her perception of the counseling relationship, counseling process, and counseling goals. The client, too, enters counseling with a certain, culturally-established value system, which impacts his or her view towards the appropriateness of counseling, the expectations for the counseling process, and the ideal counselor-client relationship. When the counselor and client value systems are the same or at least complimentary to one another, one would expect the counseling process to proceed rather smoothly. However, what happens when a client and counselor enter a counseling relationship with differing value systems?

Clearly, when a counselor and client possess markedly different value systems, the chances for therapeutic impasses and resistance increases. When counseling cross-culturally (in terms of racial/ethnic group, gender, socioeconomic status, etc.), the chances that the client and counselor enter the counseling relationship with differing values are heightened. Most counseling experts agree that to counsel effectively with any client the counselor must first be very aware of his or her own value biases, second, must be knowledgeable, sensitive, and appreciative of the client's value system, and third, must be careful not to impose his or her value system onto the client.

Unfortunately, many counseling practitioners and researchers are not aware of their own value biases (Katz, 1985; Pedersen, 1988; D.W. Sue, 1981; D.W. Sue & D. Sue, in press). Wrenn (1962, 1985) discusses the concept of "cultural encapsulation," where traditionally trained counselors are so caught up in their own belief system that they are unaware of their specific values, and they neglect to realize that there are variant, equally justifiable cultural value systems. Katz (1985) says it well when she notes:

49

... because White culture is the dominant cultural norm in the United States, it acts as an invisible veil that limits many people from seeing it as a cultural system (p. 616).

Clearly, if a counselor is culturally encapsulated, believing his or her value system to be the "model" one, then there is the strong possibility that the counselor's values will be unknowingly imposed onto the client.

Most counseling experts would agree that in most cases, the imposition of one's values (which usually happens subtly and outside the counselor's conscious awareness) onto a client is not a therapeutic goal or ideal. (There may be rare exceptions to this view, as for instance, when a client espouses a universally accepted immoral value—such as killing—in which case the counselor may indeed purposefully impose his or her values onto the client [see excellent discussion by Patterson, 1978].)

There is a general consensus among multicultural specialists that counseling training programs have neglected to give sufficient attention to the exploration of trainee values (Katz, 1985; Pedersen, 1987, 1988; Sabnani, Ponterotto, & Borodovsky, in press; D.W. Sue, 1981). Furthermore, little training emphasis has been devoted to teaching counselor trainees about the differing value systems one might encounter in counseling, particularly as predicated by racial/ethnic minority status (Benesch & Ponterotto, 1989; Parker, 1988; Pedersen, 1988; Ponterotto & Benesch, 1988; Ponterotto & Casas, 1987).

Counseling in the United States is predominantly a White middle-class phenomena; and as described in Chapter Two there is an identifiable "dominant" value system that is associated with the majority (White middle-class) group, and which pervades most current counseling training programs. Majority-group members in the U.S. are raised to believe that their value system is the most appropriate, "the best," and that people possessing non-middle-class White values should try their best to assimilate and adapt to the majority culture system. This "ethnocentric" bias has and continues to serve as a barrier to effective multicultural counseling (see Katz, 1985; Pedersen, 1988; Ponterotto, 1988a).

This chapter serves several important purposes. *First,* the current monocultural value system undergirding traditional counseling practice will be explored and specified. *Second,* the manner in which the majority value system guides the leading and most popular theories of counseling will be demonstrated. *Third,* the effects of an ethnocentric conceptual paradigm on the status of racial/ethnic minority-focused research will be explored. Finally, the importance to the counseling profession of a culturally-pluralistic research emphasis will be highlighted.

THE MONOCULTURAL BIAS OF CURRENT COUNSELING PRACTICE

Many counseling students and professionals believe that counseling is a fair, objective, and ethically-neutral phenomena. In reality, this is not the case (Casas, Ponterotto, & Gutierrez, 1986). Attitudes and values in traditional counseling practice reflect those held by the larger society. Counseling professionals constitute a subset of the larger American community, and it is logical, therefore, to expect that the sociopolitical influences affecting society as a whole will also influence counselors (Katz, 1985; Ponterotto, 1988a; D.W. Sue, 1981). Thus if society in general, has been unfair, neglectful, or even oppressive towards some racial/ethnic or other minority groups, then we can expect the counseling profession to have been, at least in part, party to this unfairness.

Most Americans would agree that the majority group in the U.S. has been unfair to certain, physically distinguishable, segments of the population. With respect to the counseling profession, one of this country's leading multicultural scholars, D.W. Sue (as identified in the Ponterotto & Sabnani, 1989 multicultural leadership survey), commented that:

> While counseling enshrines the concepts of freedom, rational thought, toler-ance of new ideas, and equality and justice for all, it can be used as an op-pressive instrument by those in power to maintain the status quo. In this respect, counseling becomes a form of oppression in which there is an unjust and cruel exercise of power to subjugate or mistreat large groups of people (D.W. Sue, 1981, p. 4).

Our perspective is that most counselors are very well-intentioned when working with any client. However, because of their "cultural encapsulation" (Wrenn, 1962, 1985), and lack of adequate multicultural training (Parker, 1988; Pedersen, 1988; Ponterotto, 1988a; Ponterotto & Casas, 1987), many counselors unknowingly impose their majority-class value system onto clients of differing cultural backgrounds. When this occurs, a counselor's well meaning behavior becomes an oppressive counseling intervention. An outcome of this counselor behavior is often client-counselor mixed communication, differential expectations for the counselor and client roles, and divergent expectations of the counseling process, all of which, collectively, lead to premature client termination from counseling and/or less than desirable counseling outcomes.

The first step in counseling effectively across cultures is to understand the value bases of the power-dominant cultural system that forms the backbone of traditional counseling training and practice (see Katz, 1985; Pedersen, 1987, 1988). Once White cultural values are identified, defined, and explored, the counselor can begin to understand the complex nature of a multicultural counseling situation.

The Majority Group Value System: A Cautionary Note

The purpose of this section is to specifically describe the White culture and explicitly delineate White cultural values. An important word of caution must be expressed first, however, before proceeding to describe any single value system. One danger of studying a particular group's value system, or comparing one group's value system to another, is the tendency to overgeneralize and stereotype particular groups. Many traditionally-trained counselors already harbor stereotypes from society's vision of racial/ethnic minorities portrayed in the media (Wilson & Gutierrez, 1985) and in the literature (see Casas, 1984). It is important not to perpetuate or further solidify stereotypical views of the majority or minority cultures. Therefore, as you read this section on White values and their differences with other groups, it is important to remember that we are talking in global and general terms.

Clearly, not every White middle-class male or female will possess the value system described below. There are many cultural differences within the White culture as within all racial/ethnic groups in the United States. Naturally, socioeconomic status differences are at times more significant than racial differences; similarly, religious, age, gender, geographical region, time living in the United States, level of acculturation, and racial identity commitment all constitute important within-group or intracultural variables that must be considered in racial/ethnic group research (see Casas, 1984).

Nevertheless, over the generations, certain core sets of values that may be interculturally distinguishable, do emerge within a particular racial/ethnic group. It is important for counselors to be familiar with general intercultural value differences commonly found in the cross-cultural research. It is equally important for counselors to know that within-group differences usually exceed between-group differences, and that no particular value system should be ascribed to a client based solely on racial group affiliation. With these cautionary notes in mind, attention is now directed to an extensive discussion on the White culture.

White Culture in the United States

As noted in Chapter Two, the majority, power dominant group in the United States is the White middle-class male (Pearson, Shavlik, & Touchton, 1989; Ponterotto, Lew, & Bullington, in press). This group has a value system that is reflected in the White House, on Wall Street, in most universities, and naturally, in counseling training programs.

Katz's (1985) definition of "White culture" first presented in Chapter Two, is presented again below to highlight the evolution and origins of the majority culture in the United States:

> White culture is the synthesis of ideas, values, and beliefs coalesced from descendants of White European ethnic groups in the United States (p. 617).

At the core of this "White value system" lies a fundamental set of values that must be understood in counseling cross-culturally. To this end, *eight* "White cultural" values that pervade current counseling theory and research have been identified and are discussed in detail in the following section. The reader interested in an expansive perspective of White American values is referred to Katz (1985), Kluckholm and Strodbeck (1961), Pedersen (1987, 1988), and Stewart (1972).

1. **Individualism.** The White culture espouses the notion of rugged individualism. The individual is seen as the primary unit of the family or group, and independence and autonomy are highly valued. Translated into counseling practice, this value is manifested by an emphasis on individual counseling; on the view that the individual has primary responsibility for events in his or her life; that personal problems are intraindividual, or rooted within the person's early childhood and family history; and that the goals of counseling should be individual-focused, such as increased autonomy and independence, and personal self-actualization.

Assuming that all Americans adhere or should adhere to this "rugged individualistic" construct would present an ethnocentric, culturally-encapsulated viewpoint. A culturally-pluralistic perspective would acknowledge that this is but one value reflection. Individuals from numerous American subcultures do not adhere to the notion of rugged individualism, and in fact some cultures devalue such a notion. Many American Indians, for example (particularly those more traditional; that is not highly acculturated into the dominant cultural system), put greater emphasis on the collective tribe than on the individual within the tribe. What is best for the tribe takes precedent over what is best for the individual. Some Hispanic subgroups, as well, put greater emphasis on the family or group than on the individual. It is essential that counselors (regardless of race) who are brought up in a White middle-class value system understand that rugged individualism is representative of one cultural group, and is by no means culturally transcendent.

2. **Competition.** The White middle-class culture is very competitive; and having a highly competitive nature is considered a valued trait. Competition is reflected in grade school, where children sit as "individual units" in desks that are arranged in rows and columns, fostering a competitive person-to-person atmosphere. Fierce competition is reflected in higher education as well as on Wall Street. Clearly, winning is very important in the dominant U.S. culture, whether the context be international politics or college sports. In counseling, this competitive perspective may be manifested on a focus of achieving self-advancing goals in preparation for the competitive world.

Compared to the White middle-class culture, some cultural/ethnic groups feel less comfortable, or even uncomfortable with competition. For many segments of the American Indian culture and Hispanic culture, for example, joint cooperative efforts are preferred to individually competitive ones. In the classroom, many less acculturated students from these ethnic groups may be more comfortable and may perform better during cooperative-oriented tasks.

3. **Achievement.** The concept of achievement is highly interrelated with those of individualism and competition. White culture is highly achievement-oriented. The greater the number of individual achievements, the greater the individual's aggregate worth to society. Achieving wealth and amassing resources bring concurrent respect and admiration. Conquering and mastering one's competitors and one's environment is considered a valuable trait.

In some racial/ethnic groups, the concept of individual achievement is not so highly valued, and in fact may be devalued. Among culturally-traditional American Indians, for example, one's integrity is measured more by how much one has given away than by how much one has accumulated. For some racial/ethnic subgroups, the achievement orientation is group focused as opposed to individual focused. For example, in the classroom, a traditional American Indian or Hispanic student may not raise his or her hand because drawing singular attention to oneself is not culturally appropriate and such an action may prove embarrassing.

4. **Time-Emphasis.** White culture is extremely time-conscious, and much of society's activities revolve around the clock, so to speak. Time is construed as linear, and being on time to a meeting or gathering is considered extremely important. In counseling, clients are expected to be exactly on time, and the counseling session is to last 50 minutes (or some predetermined time).

For some racial/ethnic groups, the White culture's emphasis on rigid time schedules seems rather absurd. Many traditional American Indians, for example, perceive time as circular, not linear, and rushing around does not make much sense. Similarly, other racial/ethnic subgroups, for example some Hispanic and Black subgroups, have less of an emphasis on rigid time adherence. Many White individuals (and minorities for that matter) jokingly refer to "C.P. Time," or "Colored People's Time," referring to the perception that people of color have more of a "laid back" approach to the time construct. Indeed, the culturally-predicated contrast of *linear time* (don't lose or waste time because it never returns) versus *circular time* (time evolves in circles, with one minute, or one day always replaced by the next, thus why rush to beat the clock?) renders a grain of truth to this stereotype.

Another aspect of the time orientation in the White culture is the emphasis on the *future*. At an early age, children are taught to work now and play later; and young adults are advised to save now to build a financial nest-egg for the future, and so on. In contrast to this perspective, an American Indian may, for example, emphasize appreciating life at the moment, and a Black family may discuss and take pride in their ancestry through the use of oral history telling.

5. **Nonverbal and Verbal Behavior.** The White middle-class culture possesses a certain accepted standard of nonverbal and verbal communication. Maintaining eye-contact while speaking, a firm handshake, and verbal expressiveness are but a few of the expected behaviors in the majority culture. As is the case with the previous values discussed, it would be erroneous to assume that individuals from varied racial/ethnic backgrounds all share this code of appropriate behavior. As an example, a recently arrived Asian American immigrant may not shake hands firmly, because such in his or her culture of origin may be a sign of

aggressiveness. Further, an American Indian client, for example, may not look his or her counselor in the eye when speaking, because such may signify disrespect. Cultural background also influences one's sense of appropriate distance between two individuals when speaking; and similarly the volume of speech or the amount of hand and other body movement may be culturally influenced.

Naturally, it is important that counselors raised in the middle-class culture not misinterpret a client's nonverbal or verbal behavior. For example, if a lower-income Black client appears to have a raised volume, this is not necessarily a sign of aggression. Similarly, an American Indian or Hispanic client who talks softly is not necessarily being defensive or resistant to the counseling process. Further, if a traditional (not highly acculturated) Asian American female client is not very verbally expressive or open to her White male counselor, she is not being uncooperative or resistant in counseling. This behavior may be a cultural reflection of not openly sharing personal information with a male outside the family structure. It goes without saying that a counselor should be familiar with the norms and expectations of the culture from which his or her client comes.

6. **Nuclear Family.** The ideal family unit in the White culture is the nuclear family arrangement. Parents live only with their children, and cousins, aunts, uncles, and grandparents live in their own nuclear family arrangements. On the other hand, some racial/ethnic subgroups are more likely to live in extended family arrangements, with parents, children, grandparents, and cousins, for example, living together, or in very close geographical proximity. Also, the involvement of relatives in family matters may also be higher in some cultural groups. For instance, the Mexican American Godfather, *Padrino*, is quite involved with his Godson, *Ahijado*, in numerous ways.

Family arrangement styles have direct implications for counseling process and research. As an example, in the traditional White culture, family counseling usually involves only the nuclear family unit, with extended family members rarely brought into the counseling process. In some racial/ethnic subgroups, however, involving extended family members in the family counseling process would be an expected course of action. As examples: it may be the appropriate course of action to invite to counseling the grandparents of an Asian American family; the tribal elder or the Shaman (Tribal healer) may be asked to participate in family counseling with an American Indian family; and for a traditional Mexican

American family it may be appropriate to invite into counseling the padrino and/or other close family relations (see Ho, 1987, for an excellent discussion of family therapy with ethnic minorities).

7. **Written Tradition.** The written word is highly valued over the spoken word in White American culture. People are always warned, "get it in writing," whatever the agreement or arrangement between two parties may entail. In some cultural groups, the spoken word, a more personal touch, is more valued than any written agreement. Breaking one's verbal oath or agreement is virtually unheard of in some groups.

Naturally, as with all the values discussed, the written emphasis may have implications for counseling. For instance, a traditional, reservation-dwelling American Indian may be taken aback by a counselor's suggestion of forming a written counseling contract specifying counseling goals and timelines.

In the realm of research, the cultural implication of this "written" value comes quite sharply into focus. The counseling profession, and the academic university that houses counseling departments, puts high emphasis on written history and research—clearly a Western-European notion (see Katz, 1985). Oral histories, on the other hand, are given less academic credibility, yet this method of generation-to-generation knowledge acquisition plays an important role in the American Indian tribal culture, and among many Black families in the U.S.

8. **Scientific Method.** Strongly influenced by the European empirico-scientific tradition, the White culture in the United States emphasizes the value of "hard science" and its associated research methodologies. The quantitative, atomistic (examining minute aspects of a phenomena) bias of research published in our profession's most respected journal, the *Journal of Counseling Psychology,* has been noted previously and discussed at length (see Goldman, 1976; Ponterotto, 1988b).

Some multicultural scholars (e.g., Helms, 1989a) note that this quantitative emphasis extant in the counseling literature is sometimes at cross-purposes with the study of culture, which is a complex construct (Pedersen, 1988) that may be more reliably studied using a variety of research methods (to be discussed more fully in Chapters Seven and Nine). A number of multicultural writers (e.g., Ponterotto, 1988b, 1989) believe that although the quantitative emphasis incorporating the minute examination of large group differences is of value, multicultural research could be greatly augmented with the incorporation of qualitative, small-group designs common in the field of anthropology. Qualitative methods such as field observations, ethnographic reports, oral histories, and single-case studies could be of great value in multicultural counseling research (see Chapter Nine).

Values Discussion Summary

As noted at the beginning of this section on values, there is always the danger of perpetuating ethnic categorizations and stereotypes when values are discussed on a global, intercultural level. It is important to emphasize that there are probably more cultural and value differences *within* any single racial/ethnic subgroup than between any two groups. Notwithstanding this caution, it is important for counselors to study and incorporate *possible* culture-specific value tendencies when working multiculturally, whether in clinical practice or in research.

It must be emphasized again, that within groups, variables such as acculturation level (see Padilla, 1980; Padilla & Lindholm, 1984; Padilla & Salgado De Snyder, 1985; Ponterotto, 1987) and racial identity development (see Helms, 1990; Parham, 1989) are essential components for accurately understanding and assisting clients from respective racial/ethnic minority groups and subgroups. With this understanding of intercultural values in general, and the acknowledgement of the centrality of intracultural differences to understanding a particular racial/ethnic group, it is now appropriate to examine how and why traditional theories of counseling may be fundamentally biased.

THE NATURE OF CULTURAL BIAS IN COUNSELING THEORY

In recent years, extensive criticism has been leveled at traditional theories of counseling vis-a-vis their appropriateness and effectiveness with persons from racial/ethnic minority groups. Numerous multicultural scholars in counseling maintain that Western-based counseling systems were developed by and for individuals of Euro-Anglo background, particularly the White middle and upper-middle classes (see Atkinson et al., 1989; Katz, 1985), and that consequently these theories are socioculturally-biased and may not be appropriate for many segments of the non-White population (Benesch & Ponterotto, 1989; Casas & Vasquez, 1989; Ponterotto, 1987; D.W. Sue, 1981).

Using the preceding discussion on White cultural values as a contextual base, it is not difficult to understand why multicultural critics perceive traditional counseling theories as ethno-culturally biased. The major goal of this section will be to specifically examine how traditional theories or systems of counseling manifest their cultural bias.

No theory develops in a vacuum. Theories originate and grow within specific sociocultural contexts. Most leading theories of counseling taught in hundreds of counseling training programs throughout the United States were founded and developed by individuals with ancestry in Europe. Thus the philosophical assumptions of these theories, along with their concomitant value and attitude components naturally reflect a Euro-Anglo cultural perspective.

There are many specific theories of counseling, and probably each could be criticized from a racial/ethnic minority perspective. To demonstrate this fact, three general theoretical counseling models that are reflective of theory training curriculum in the United States are critiqued from a racial/ethnic minority perspective in the following section. These three theories are psychoanalytic, existential-humanistic, and behavioral.

Psychoanalytic Theories of Counseling

Psychoanalysis, a system of psychology stemming from the work of Sigmund Freud, emphasizes the importance of unconscious forces in directing the individual's mental life. Other systems of counseling with a psychodynamic basis include the schools of thought established by Alfred Adler and Carl Jung. Psychodynamic theories of counseling extend the rationalist spirit of Greek philosophy in its command to "know thyself." In the psychodynamic conception, individual problems are viewed as residing within one's self and rooted in early childhood experiences with significant others (see comprehensive overview by Arlow, 1989). Goals of psychodynamic-focused counseling stress the uncovering, processing, and working through of unconscious mental forces driving behavior and thoughts.

Psychodynamic theories of counseling have been harshly criticized from a minority perspective because they emphasize the importance of intrapsychic variables and give little attention to sociocultural variables (e.g., racism, oppression) outside the client's control (Atkinson et al., 1989; Ponterotto, 1987). Critics of the psychodynamic approaches comment that many concerns of racial/ethnic minorities are not in their realm of control, and thus intrapsychic examination will serve little pragmatic benefit. Minorities in this country are often confronted, both in blatant and subtle ways, with social injustices and prejudicial views; therefore a change is needed not in the clients' psyches but in the environment in which these people live and work.

In regards to the psychodynamic therapeutic process, clients are expected to be verbal and self-disclosing. This therapeutic process is fine for a culture that values verbal expression, such as the White middle-class culture; but such therapeutic activity may be very alien to a traditional Asian American client, for example, who is taught not to disclose feelings and not to be particularly verbal with nonfamily members.

Existential-Humanistic Theories of Counseling

Counseling theories that would fall under the rubric of existential-humanistic counseling include Carl Rogers's Person-Centered approach, Frederick Perls's Gestalt approach, Eugene Gendlin's Experiential counseling, and Viktor Frankl's Logotherapeutic system, among others (see various chapters in Corsini & Wedding, 1989). Connecting links between these individual models of counseling are the focus on *present experiencing* as opposed to a *past* emphasis; the importance of the counseling relationship in which the counselor is empathic, caring, genuine, and nonjudgemental; and where central goals of counseling include increased individual autonomy, independence, and self-actualization.

Existential-humanistic approaches to counseling focus on the client's awareness, growth, self-acceptance, self-esteem, and self-actualization. This person-centered emphasis is appropriate for the White middle-class culture with its emphasis on individuation and autonomy. This counseling emphasis, however, may cause extensive stress and guilt in a client who comes from a cultural group that de-emphasizes individualism and stresses instead the collective importance of family, community, or tribe. For example, whereas career-oriented counseling for an Anglo client may stress personal goals, abilities, and vocational interests, for a first generation Asian American it may be more appropriate to stress parental goals for the children, expectations for the eldest child, and familial patterns of vocations passed along generationally (see Suinn, 1985).

Behavioral Approaches to Counseling

Behavioral approaches to counseling postulate that maladaptive behavior patterns are learned, and therefore can be unlearned. This therapeutic system incorporates operant and classical learning paradigms to modify inappropriate and maladaptive behavior and thought patterns. In behavioral counseling, the counselor-client relationship parallels that of teacher-learner, and the approach is basically psychoeducational. In relation to the *time* perspective, behavioral counseling focuses on the present and future of the client's life, not the past.

Of the three general orientations to counseling, the behavioral approach has received the most positive commentary vis a vis racial/ethnic minority appropriateness (see Casas, 1976). In summarizing the behavioral approaches with Mexican Americans, Ponterotto (1987) comments that:

> This action-oriented, problem-solving approach has been deemed more appropriate for [racial/ethnic minorities] because it involves activating one's role in the environment and, when possible, activating the environment itself (p. 308).

One advantage of the behavioral model is that counseling is guided by a contractual agreement between both client and counselor, specifying the goals and methods of intervention. This active participation on the part of the clients can be beneficial because it allows them to select counseling goals and techniques that are not contrary to cultural norms and expectations.

Although viewed more favorably (than psychodynamic and existential-humanistic approaches) by a number of racial/ethnic minority-focused scholars, the behavioral approach is also highly encapsulated in a White middle-class value system. For instance, behavioral counseling stresses a future goal orientation with an emphasis on temporal aspects of the counseling process (e.g., setting time limits in which to reach agreed upon goals). This emphasis on a future time perspective, a *linear* view, is at odds with clients who may have a cultural trait of time that is *circular.* Many American Indians who are culturally traditional may find a futuristic counseling emphasis somewhat confusing and culturally alien.

THE CULTURAL BIAS OF TRADITIONAL COUNSELING RESEARCH

Chapter One introduced a number of concerns directed at the past and current status of psychological research on racial/ethnic minorities. This section of Chapter Five discusses the bias of traditional counseling research as reflected in an extension of the White middle-class value system.

Recent years have witnessed intense criticism of the objectivity, relativity, and utility of psychological research on racial/ethnic minority populations (Casas, 1985a; Ponterotto, 1988b; S. Sue, 1988). Influential multicultural scholars (e.g., Katz, 1985; D.W. Sue, 1981) have isolated three conceptual models that have guided past research on racial/ethnic minorities, and are, in part, responsible for the poor status of such research. The three models are the *pathological model*, the *genetically-deficient model*, and the *culturally-deficient or deprived model* (see D.W. Sue, 1981 primarily, and Casas, 1985b, and Katz, 1985 secondarily).

Pathological Model

D.W. Sue (1981) and A. Thomas and Sillen (1972) believe that an underlying assumption held by many early psychological researchers was that minorities, particularly Blacks, were somewhat pathological, or in other terms, less psychologically healthy than Whites. With this racist belief in hand, many researchers undertook experiments testing their assumptions about minorities. Citing the work of A. Thomas and Sillen (1972), D.W. Sue (1981) cites several early historical research examples perpetuating this bias:

1. Fabricated 1840 census figures supported the notion "that Blacks living under unnatural conditions of freedom were prone to anxiety" (D.W. Sue, 1981, p. 12).
2. Mentally-healthy Blacks were content with subservience.
3. Given the simplicity of the Black mind, they were less likely to become mentally ill.
4. The dreams of Blacks were more simple and less complex than those of White people.

Another issue to consider when examining the pathological bias of minority research is the mechanism for assessing *pathology*. Many of these early studies used psychological assessments normed on the White middle-class culture. When these assessments were indiscriminately used with some racial/ethnic groups, the collective results painted a picture of Blacks being more neurotic, anxious, paranoid, and psychotic than their White counterparts (D.W. Sue, 1981).

Genetically-Deficient Model

This model holds that Blacks and other racial/ethnic minority groups are biologically inferior to Whites with regards to intellectual capacity (See Katz, 1985; D.W. Sue, 1981). Again, citing the work of A. Thomas and Sillen (1972), D.W. Sue (1981) presents the results of early research fostering this genetically-based research bias.

1. The brain of a Black person is smaller and less developed than that of a White person.
2. Influential medical journals fostered the stereotype that Blacks were less anatomically, neurologically, and endocrinologically developed than Whites.

(Note: D.W. Sue [1981] included these two examples under the pathological model, however, given their genetic basis, we include them under the genetic model.)

This genetic-deficiency-based conception stimulated extensive research measuring and comparing the intelligence levels of various racial/ethnic groups. Naturally, most of the early intelligence tests were developed with a White middle-class conceptual base and therefore were biased towards non-White groups. Casas (1985b), Katz (1985), and D.W. Sue (1981) comment that the genetically-deficient model was evident in the professional literature up until the late 1960s and early 1970s (e.g., Jensen, 1969; Shockley, 1971; Shuey, 1966).

Culturally-Deprived Model

Concerned with the negative view of minorities portrayed in the genetically-deficient model, well-meaning researchers began to refer to the minority cultures as deprived. This conception effectively served to move the cause of "minority inferiority" out of the genes and into the "disadvantaged" cultural environment. This model held that racial/ethnic minorities tended to succeed less frequently in school, in the home (i.e., marital and family stability), and at work, because they, more likely than Whites, grew up in poorer neighborhoods where environmental factors such as poor living conditions, lack of proper cognitive stimulation (e.g., books), and lack of positive role models would render them at a great disadvantage for competing in the larger society (see Smith, 1977; D.W. Sue, 1981).

With the culturally-deprived model as a conceptual base, researchers would go into the minority community attempting to study what was wrong with the culture (e.g., Moynihan, 1965); and attempt to discern what it might take to make it "right"—that is, like the White middle-class culture. Naturally, this research emphasis, although less distasteful than the genetically-deficient model, still places all the blame for segregated racial conditions on the minority culture, and does not examine the culture's interaction with the power dominant White culture (see Casas, 1985b).

In a strong argument, D.W. Sue (1981) summarizes the results of the practice and underlying data base of counseling as follows: "(a) subjugation of the culturally different, (b) perpetuation of the view that minorities are inherently pathological, (c) perpetuation of racist practices in counseling, and (d) provision of an excuse to the profession for not taking social action to rectify inequities in the system" (pp. 19–20).

A CULTURALLY-PLURALISTIC RESEARCH PERSPECTIVE

Research conducted in recent years has moved from studying minorities as culturally-pathological, deficient, or deprived to studying them as *different* from the White middle-class culture. Clearly the *culturally-different* model is preferred to the earlier models described (Baratz & Baratz, 1970; D.W. Sue, 1981). Katz (1985), in reviewing the various conceptual models for psychological research on minorities, comments that:

> The culturally different model assumes that minorities are neither deviant, pathological, nor inferior. It does, however, acknowledge that minorities in the United States are bicultural and function in at least two different cultural contexts simultaneously. Individuals are viewed in relation to their environment, with a pragmatic recognition of racism and its effect upon varied racial groups (pp. 620–621).

Despite the consensus that the culturally-different model is naturally preferred to the culturally-pathological, deficient, or deprived models, we still are somewhat concerned with semantics. In the United States, being "different" subtly implies less than or not on the same level. Take the phrase, "they're just different than us" as an example. Here the word "different" still has a negative connotation. Perhaps one immediate goal for counseling researchers is to establish semantically-neutral terminology with regards to conceptual paradigms. Perhaps *culturally-variable*, or *culturally-diverse*, could be used instead of *culturally-different.*

Terminology must be developed that emphasizes the richness and value of cultural diversity in this country. We feel similarly about the term "minority." Being a minority implies that one is not in the norm; it sends the subtle message that the majority culture is the one to be emulated. As discussed in Chapter One, developing consistent, semantically-neutral terminology for the young field of multicultural counseling is one of our tasks (see Gelso et al., 1988).

The final section of this chapter presents three more general suggestions for culturally-pluralistic research. The reader is reminded that Chapter Eleven is devoted exclusively to future directions for racial/ethnic minority counseling research.

1. There is a need to study the positive aspects of racial/ethnic minority cultures. For instance, one can study the advantages of being bicultural (see Casas, 1984; D.W. Sue, 1981). A more balanced research agenda examining both positive aspects and stressors faced by racial/ethnic groups is needed.

2. One dominant value in the White middle-class culture is the heavy emphasis on the strict scientific method, including rational and linear thinking, dualistic interpretations, cause and effect relationships, and a quantitative emphasis (Katz, 1985). Casas (1985a), Patterson (1972), D.W. Sue (1981), and Ponterotto (1988b, 1989) note that this atomistic research emphasis has hindered research dealing with complex social and psychological problems facing humankind. The study of culture is quite complex (Pedersen, 1988), and various methodologies are needed to study the construct (see Helms, 1989a, 1989b). Research is needed that is conceptual and theory building on the one hand (Ponterotto, 1988b), and that is pragmatic and immediately useful on the other hand (Smith, Burlew, Mosley, & Whitney, 1978). Smith et al. (1978) comment that racial/ethnic minority mental health research:

> . . . should focus on changing the social conditions and systems which impinge on mental-health functioning. By focusing on the systemic issues and conditions that contribute to the mental-health behavior of minorities, we may be able to develop preventive models and strategies and thus improve their mental-health functioning (p. 178).

3. Researchers studying racial/ethnic minority populations have been criticized for not collaborating with the minority communities in which they conduct their investigations (Gordon, 1973; Ponterotto, 1988b; D.W. Sue, 1981; C.W. Thomas, 1970). Working with community leaders and involving minorities in all aspects of the research endeavor are important components of ethically considerate and professionally conducive

research (Atkinson et al., 1989; Ponterotto, 1988b). This topic is addressed at greater length in Chapter Ten.

CONCLUSION

This chapter has reviewed the conceptual bias reflected in past counseling practice, training, and research. The evidence is strong that traditional counseling methods perpetuate the societal and political status quo (see also Atkinson et al., 1989; Halleck, 1971; D.W. Sue & S. Sue, 1972). The White cultural system and its concurrent value emphases were specifically defined and discussed. Three major theoretical approaches to counseling were reviewed and critiqued from a culturally-pluralistic perspective. Conceptual models guiding past research in racial/ethnic minority counseling were discussed and critiqued. Finally, a general call for a renewed, pluralistic, multicultural research agenda was made.

The subsequent chapters of this book take a more focused look at past and present research in the field. Chapter Six presents a topical review of recent empirical research in racial/ethnic minority counseling. Chapter Seven then identifies major research criticisms noted in the literature and determines their validity through a systematic assessment of recent empirical studies. Chapters Eight through Ten extend some of the points made in the preceding section (the Pluralistic Research Perspective) and specifically guide the reader in the conduct of both quantitative and qualitative research on minorities; on how to access and work with the minority community; and on how to ensure the highest standard of professional ethics when working with racial/ethnic minority populations.

Chapter Six

RECENT RESEARCH IN RACIAL/ETHNIC MINORITY COUNSELING: A TOPICAL REVIEW

In line with the objectives inherent in this handbook, this chapter focuses on the major racial/ethnic minority topics that have been covered in articles recently published in professional journals. More specifically, this chapter reports the results of a recent content analysis of articles published in four major counseling journals—*The Counseling Psychologist, Journal of Counseling Psychology, Journal of Counseling and Development,* and *Journal of Multicultural Counseling and Development,* covering the period from 1983 to 1988. This six-year, four-journal content analysis identified 183 conceptual and empirical articles focusing on racial/ethnic minority populations. The first part of this chapter presents a topical analysis of these articles and organizes them into major categories. Using this content analysis as a base, the latter part of the chapter presents a conceptual framework to help researchers and practitioners alike to evaluate the heuristic and, more importantly, the pragmatic, utilitarian value of the respective topics within the context of the total counseling process.

As a result of the aforementioned analysis, it was found that the myriad of topics addressed in the 183 articles could be placed into one of the following five broad categories: client variables, counselor variables, counseling process variables, assessment, and professional issues and development. From a historical perspective, it should be noted that these categories, with the exception of professional issues and development, are similar to those that were identified as applicable for use in a comparable review that included a more extensive selection of counseling-related journals and that covered the five-year period between 1980 and 1984 (see Casas, 1984). The necessity to add a professional issues and development category reflects the increased number of articles that focus on training and development programs as well as issues of direct relevance to racial/ethnic minorities.

67

Relative to the distribution of articles across categories, the largest number of articles, sixty, was found under the category of client variables, demonstrating a growing professional need to develop a more in-depth and comprehensive understanding of the racial/ethnic minority client. The rest of the articles are distributed among the other categories in the following descending order: counseling process, professional issues and development, assessment, and counselor variables.

With respect to the representation of the respective racial/ethnic groups across all categories, articles that focus on Black clients and/or issues are much more prevalent in the literature. In fact, the total number of articles on Blacks is more than the combined number of articles that focus on the other three racial/ethnic minority groups. In addition, while the articles focusing on Blacks are found in the five categories noted above, the same does not hold true for the other groups. The number of articles on Hispanics and Asian Americans, depending on category, continues to be fairly moderate to low, while the number of articles on Native Americans is almost nonexistent. Interestingly, the few articles on Native Americans focus on presenting problems and more specifically those having a psychopathological nature (e.g., alcoholism, depression, suicide, substance abuse).

What follows is a brief overview of the subcategories and topics that are contained within each of the five categories.

CLIENT VARIABLES

This category encompasses quite a diverse array of topics and thus for the sake of organization it is necessary to break it down into subcategories that are presented in order of their representativeness in the literature:

Sociocultural Characteristics

Given the aforementioned need to develop a more comprehensive understanding of the racial/ethnic minority client, it is not surprising that the topics included under this broad subcategory are quite diverse in nature. This being the case, for the sake of organization, it is necessary to break this subcategory down into four general topical areas.

The first topical area encompasses those articles that direct attention to behaviors and social patterns associated with specific sociocultural values, attitudes, and customs: for example, assertiveness (Fukuyama &

Greenfield, 1983; Garrison & Jenkins, 1986; D. Sue, Ino, & Sue, 1983); self-disclosure (Molina & Franco, 1986); social support systems (Stewart & Vaux, 1986); dating patterns (Clark, Windley, Jones, & Ellis, 1986); identifying Black university student's personal problem-solving styles (Reeder & Heppner, 1985); profiling Hispanic women in higher education (Casas & Ponterotto, 1984); examining study habits and academic achievement in higher education (Francis & Kelly, 1988; Lunneburg & Lunneburg, 1986; Sue & Zane, 1985); measuring the attitudes of Navajo children towards nontraditional occupations (Beyard-Tyler & Haring, 1984); exploring factors that influence the career goals of Black women (Thomas, 1986); and examining psychosocial reasons for interracial relationships (Pope, 1986).

The second topical area focuses on those articles that address sociopsychological developmental constructs that are the products of past history, personal experiences, and sociocultural factors: assessing racial identity and acculturation and their impact on varied behaviors and affective states (Parham & Helms, 1985b; Sodowsky & Carey, 1988); identifying existing levels of self-esteem and self-actualization (Asamen & Berry, 1987; Gardner, 1985; Hoffman & Hale-Benson, 1987; Parham & Helms, 1985b); and examining Hispanic adult developmental and adjustment levels (Ross, 1984).

The third area contains articles that identify specific problems and/or groups that need to be understood within their racial/ethnic minority context: gifted adolescents (Lindstrom & Van Sant, 1986); at-risk Black men (Parham & McDavis, 1987); Black battered women (Coley & Beckett, 1988); Black deaf children (Stewart & Benson, 1988); general problems presented by Asian-American students (Tracey, Leong, & Glidden, 1986); alcoholism (Gade & Hurlburt, 1985); attempted suicides (Thurman, Martin, & Martin, 1985); depression (Gary & Berry, 1985); and substance abuse (Kirk, 1986; Pedigo, 1983).

Finally, the fourth area, which contains much fewer articles, encompasses articles that address historical factors and mainstream White attitudes that impact racial/ethnic minorities: historical factors that still have direct and/or indirect impact on the functioning of minorities (Henkin, 1985); and measuring White attitudes towards Blacks and Hispanics (White & Sedlacek, 1987).

Counselor Preference and Effectiveness

The articles that fall under this subcategory can be placed under two major topics. The first topic addresses the impact of specific client characteristics (i.e., race, ethnicity, gender, racial identity, acculturation level and/or attitude similarity) on attitude towards satisfaction with and perceived effectiveness of counseling (e.g., Atkinson, Ponce, & Martinez, 1984; Atkinson, Winzelberg, & Holland, 1985; Berg & Wright, 1988; Lee, Sutton, Honore, & Uhlemann, 1983; Neimeyer & Gonzales, 1983; Pomales, Claiborn, & LaFromboise, 1986; Terrell & Terrell, 1984). The second topic broadly encompasses client preferences for one or more of the following counselor characteristics: race, ethnicity, sex, religion, educational background, attitudes, values, age, personality, experience, and preferred counseling style (Atkinson, Furlong, & Poston, 1986; Bernstein, Wade, & Hofmann, 1987; Haviland, Horswill, O'Connell, Dynneson, 1983; Ponterotto, Alexander, Hinkston, 1988; Ponterotto, Anderson, & Grieger, 1986; Sanchez & Atkinson, 1983).

Client Expectations

In line with its title, the articles placed under this subcategory essentially focus on the general expectations that minorities hold relative to the counseling process: for example, expectations regarding formality, directiveness, and the degree of openness and self-disclosure for both client and counselor (Cherbosque, 1987; Taussig, 1987); and/or the impact that the client's characteristics (e.g., race, gender) may have on impressions and expectations of a counselor with varied attributes (e.g., race, ethnicity, gender, attractiveness; Green, Cunningham, & Yanico, 1986).

COUNSELING PROCESS

Given the broadness of this category, it is not surprising that the topics included herein are quite diverse in nature. The topics cover interventions that are based on a variety of theoretical models, for example: psychoanalytic (Brandell, 1988); existential (Vontress, 1988); systemic (Gunnings & Lipscomb, 1986); multimodal (Ponterotto, 1987); self-directed (Gade, Fuqua, & Hurlburt, 1984); group therapy (Shipp, 1983); and indigenous models (Das, 1987; Ishiyama, 1987).

A number of articles under this category focus on special interventions for specific groups, for example: Black males (Larrabee, 1986); Japanese American children (Tomine, 1985); at-risk students (Smith & McMillon, 1986); the biracial child (Brandell, 1988); and unprepared students (J. Jackson, 1987). Focused attention is also directed at training or skill building interventions, for example: social skills/assertiveness training (Huey & Rank, 1984; LaFromboise & Rowe, 1983; Stewart & Lewis, 1986); career planning and development (Obleton, 1984; Perry & Locke, 1985; Rodriguez & Blocher, 1988); leadership training (Young, 1986); bicultural competence skills (Schinke, Orlandi, Botvin, Gilchrest, Trimble, & Locklear, 1988). Finally, innovative ways to improve counseling or educational service delivery to the "evasive" racial/ethnic minority client are presented (Cole, Thomas, & Lee, 1988; June, 1986; Palacios & Franco, 1986; Tidwell, 1988).

As evident, the topics included in this subcategory are quite diverse, however, a common thread that runs throughout all the articles is the need to give accurate and appropriate attention to the client's sociocultural reality throughout any and all parts of the counseling process.

PROFESSIONAL ISSUES AND DEVELOPMENT

The need to add this category to those used in previous reviews of the literature reflects a strong and conscientious effort to make the profession aware of relevant ethical issues associated with the provision of effective counseling to minorities as well as providing guidelines and models to train counselors to provide such services. More specifically, the articles that focus on issues address the ethical need to make training, research, and service more responsive to the needs of racial/ethnic minority persons (e.g., Cayleff, 1986). To underscore this need, several articles focus on the lack of specific attention directed to minorities in the ethical principles and guidelines that serve to direct and govern all aspects of the profession, including training and research (Casas, Ponterotto, & Gutierrez, 1986; Chikezie, 1984; Ibrahim & Arredondo, 1986; Ponterotto & Casas, 1987).

The largest number of articles that fall under this category focus on presenting training models that can help counselors to improve their abilities vis-a-vis the minority client: for example, racial consciousness training model (Ponterotto, 1988a); dyadic encounter training model (Beale, 1986); triadic training model (Neimeyer, Fukuyama, Bingham, Hall, & Mussenden, 1985); and training models that integrate content with cultural sensitivity, self-awareness and practical experience (Margolis & Rungta, 1986; Merta, Stringham, & Ponterotto, 1988). Demonstrating a strong sensitivity to the changing demographics (see Chapters Two and Three) several articles addressed future directions that the profession needs to consider with respect to racial/ethnic minorities (Heath, Neimeyer, & Pedersen, 1988; M.L. Jackson, 1987).

ASSESSMENT

In the previous review of the literature described above (Casas, 1984), testing and assessment was addressed as a subcategory of the counseling process category; however, in the interim since that review was published, the number of articles focusing on test development and assessment has increased enough to warrant a separate category. Though a variety of reasons could be given to explain this increase, one that merits attention given the focus of this book is the fact that a growing number of counselors are becoming sensitive to the need to develop culturally appropriate assessment approaches (e.g., Gregory & Lee, 1986) and instruments or to validate existing instruments for use with racial/ethnic minorities and as per the articles reviewed, this is especially true with respect to vocational, career, and interest inventories.

Reflecting this career focus, the majority of articles report studies conducted to determine the applicability of vocational theory as well as general process and personality-based theories and constructs to racial/ethnic minorities (e.g., Gade, Fuqua, & Hurlburt, 1988; Henry, Bardo, Mouro, & Bryson, 1987; Leonard, 1985; Walsh, Woods, & Ward, 1986). A number of studies in this category also focused on the concurrent, convergent and/or construct validity of varied vocational interest instruments vis-a-vis racial/ethnic minorities (e.g., Fouad, Cudeck, & Hansen, 1984; Sheffey, Bingham, & Walsh, 1986). Similar studies are also reported for less traditional and/or innovative inventories (e.g., Revised Student Developmental Task Inventory, Itzkowitz & Petrie, 1988; the Racial Identity Attitude Scale, Ponterotto & Wise, 1987).

COUNSELOR VARIABLES

Unlike the increase in articles that warranted the addition of the assessment category, this category was almost eliminated due to the sparcity of articles dealing with counselor variables. Although only three articles merited inclusion in this category (Bishop & Richards, 1987; McIntyre & Pernell, 1985; Pedersen, 1987), the topic they addressed is of such importance to counselors that they warrant mention in this review. Reflecting an ethical concern that has been receiving greater attention over the years (see Casas, 1984), these three articles focused on the impact that counselor biases relative to race/ethnicity can have on the provision of mental health and educational services to minority clients.

Finally, the few other significant articles that do not fall under the purview of the categories listed above and that are directly tied to the increased availability of publications consisted of general or racial/ethnic minority group specific topical reviews or analyses of relevant publications (e.g., Atkinson, 1985; Leong, 1986; Ponterotto, 1986; Ponterotto, 1988b). A recent publication that merits mention because of the rich information that it contains is a review of the career counseling literature as it relates to Hispanics written by Arbona (1990).

The increase in the diversity of articles relative to and relevant for racial/ethnic minorities might lead some to conclude that the counseling profession is making significant strides towards addressing the research and, concomitantly, the training and service needs of racial/ethnic minorities. Unfortunately, such a conclusion is too premature at this time. There is no question that the number and diversity of articles relative to racial/ethnic minorities has increased; however, they continue to fall short from a lack of a theoretical guiding framework as well as from the perspective of methodological quality.

A CONCEPTUAL FRAMEWORK FOR INTEGRATING RESEARCH AND PRACTICE

The concern for the lack of a theoretical/structural framework has only recently been addressed in the literature (Casas & Vasquez, 1989; Ponterotto, 1988b). This concern essentially focuses on the fact that while research studies have increased, there has been no existing framework from which researchers and practitioners can evaluate the heuristic and, more importantly, the pragmatic, utilitarian value of the respective studies. Thus, while one study underscores the importance of understanding the family structure of the racial/ethnic minority client, another enthusiastically identifies an effective technique to use with these clients in general. Such information may have value, but greater value would accrue if a framework existed that enabled the reader to determine the relative importance of the information vis-a-vis the total and dynamic counseling process. Lacking such a framework, much of the information available in the literature has been inappropriately understood and evaluated and, in turn, used ineffectively with the racial/ethnic minority client. Finally, from a pragmatic research perspective, lacking such a framework makes it extremely difficult to identify those areas or topics that should be given research priority.

Addressing this concern for a lack of a guiding theoretical framework, Casas and Vasquez (1989) proposed a framework that presents categorical variables along a continuum, starting with those more covert and distal to the counseling process and progressing toward those proximic variables that are more integral to the process. Table IX represents an extension of the framework proposed by Casas & Vasquez (1989). As evident in the Table, starting with the distal variables, the first category enumerates selective personal and professional sociocultural characteristics, beliefs, attitudes, and behaviors inherent to the counselor and strongly affecting the cross-cultural counseling process. The second category focuses on the client. More specifically, it identifies personal sociocultural characteristics and variables including beliefs and attitudes and life experiences that *must* be understood and appropriately addressed in the counseling process. Finally, the third category encompasses interacting client and counselor variables including expectations, preferences, and attitudes, and counseling specific behaviors and skills that in unison are an intricate part of the counseling process itself and as such merit *serious* consideration and understanding.

With respect to the recent research reviewed in this chapter, it should be noted that the proposed theoretical framework quite aptly encompasses the categorical foci of the preponderance of articles that are presently being published including the training-focused articles that fall under the "professional issues and development" category. Given its comprehensiveness, researchers should find the use of this framework within the context of the information contained throughout this book very helpful in their efforts to identify the focus of past studies, assess the methodological type, range, and quality of these studies, and finally determine those areas that urgently require further work.

Table IX.
Theoretical Framework for Understanding the Cross-Cultural Counseling Process

SELECTIVE COUNSELOR VARIABLES		SELECTIVE CLIENT VARIABLES		SELECTIVE COUNSELING PROCESS VARIABLES	
PERSONAL SOCIO-CULTURAL	PROFESSIONAL	PERSONAL SOCIO-CULTURAL	LIFE EXPERIENCES	CLIENT	COUNSELOR (SETTING & TREATMENT)
Biological/Psych. Predisposition Gender Race Sexual Preference Life Experiences Culture Assumptions/World Views Beliefs Values Attitudes Cognitive Styles Information Processing Biased Thinking Stereotyping Self-Perception Racial Identity Acculturation Level Racial Consciousness & Sensitivity Behaviors	Culture Assumptions Beliefs Values Attitudes Training Philosophy Theoretical Orientation Basic Counseling Skills Cross-Cultural Coun. Skills Behaviors	Biological/Psych. Predisposition Gender Race Sexual Preference Culture Assumptions/World Views Beliefs Values Attitudes Cognitive Styles Information Processing Biased Thinking Stereotyping Self-Perception Self-Esteem Self-Efficacy Racial Identity Acculturation Level Aptitudes, Abilities, Interests Hopes & Expectations Behaviors	Place of Birth Nationality-Immigrant Status (For self & family members) Reasons for Immigrating Ethnicity-Visible Characteristics Socio-Economic Status Employment History Family Characteristics Level of Acculturation Type: Single/Two Parent, Extended Number of Children Child Rearing Practices Living Environment Stability & Type Urban/Rural Segregated/Integrated Safety Available Support Systems Educational History Social/Political/Economic Stressors Health Status: Physical & Mental Access to & Use of Relevant Services	Expectations of Counseling Process Counselor Role/Attributes Client Role Preferences for Counselor Approach/Technique Race-Level of Racial Identity Ethnicity – Level of Acculturation Personality Attributes Attitudes Towards Counseling Process Counselor Race/Ethnicity & Personal Attributes Credibility Attributed to Counseling Process Perceived Nature of Presenting Problem Follow-Through, Termination, Outcome	Setting Location, Accessibility Ambience Staffing: Racial, Ethnic, Gender, Linguistic Composition Level of Sensitivity to Personal & Professional Biases & Stereotypes Understanding & Respecting Client's Culture Understanding Client's Expectations, Preferences & Attitudes Accepting the Intra & Extra Psychic Nature of Presenting Probs. Establishing Credibility Building Rapport Selecting Effective/Appropriate Interventions Follow-Through, Termination, Outcome

DISTAL   PROXIMIC

CONCLUSION

As evident in this and other earlier reviews of the literature (see Casas, 1984), the 1980s have witnessed an increase in the diversity of articles relative to racial/ethnic minorities. Unfortunately, as previously mentioned, these articles have fallen short from a lack of a theoretical guiding framework as well as from the perspective of methodological quality. As noted above, with respect to the concern relative to the lack of a guiding framework, efforts have recently been extended to develop a prototype of such a framework which if utilized by researchers should help to give shape and direction to their future research efforts (see Casas, Vasquez, Barón, & Ponterotto, in preparation).

With respect to the concern for methodological quality, Chapter Seven takes the same articles reviewed from a topical perspective in this chapter and critically examines them from the perspective of methodology. Building on the information provided in Chapter Seven, Chapters Eight and Nine focus on steps that can be taken to improve the methodological quality of future research endeavors. Finally, Chapter Ten directs attention to the need for research that not only relates but is also relevant to the needs of racial/ethnic minorities.

Chapter Seven

RESEARCH METHODOLOGY IN RACIAL/ETHNIC MINORITY COUNSELING: A SYSTEMATIC CRITIQUE AND ASSESSMENT

In the last two decades increasing attention has been paid to racial/ethnic minority issues in counseling (Ponterotto, 1988b). Despite this increased attention, a number of multicultural counseling specialists (e.g., Atkinson & Schein, 1986; Casas, 1984, 1985a; D.W. Sue, 1981, 1989; D.W. Sue & D. Sue, in press; S. Sue, 1988) have been critical of the status of past and recent research in the field. Concern has been raised over the validity and applied pragmatic utility of the many research findings now appearing in the racial/ethnic minority literature. In fact, one recent article went so far as to ethically and professionally indict the counseling profession for its research failures relative to minority populations (cf. Casas, Ponterotto, & Gutierrez, 1986).

For the results of research to be meaningful and useful, the methodologies used to conduct the research must be valid and reliable. Many of the recent criticisms leveled at racial/ethnic minority counseling research center on important issues of methodology. The focus of this chapter is on issues and criticisms related to counseling research on racial/ethnic minority populations. The major purpose of the chapter is threefold:

1. To identify and describe frequently cited criticisms of multicultural counseling research.

2. To assess the validity of these criticisms against a systematically accumulated data base.

3. To provide conceptual and methodological suggestions for research in racial/ethnic minority counseling.

An examination of recent literature (including Atkinson, 1983, 1985; Atkinson & Schein, 1986; Casas, 1984, 1985a, 1985b; Casas et al., 1986; Gordon, 1973; Pedersen, 1988; Ponterotto, 1988b, 1989; Smith, Burlew, Mosley, & Whitney, 1978; D.W. Sue, 1981; D.W. Sue & D. Sue, in press; S. Sue, 1988; S. Sue, Akutsu, & Higashi, 1985; Suinn, 1985; among others) reveals a cluster of frequently noted racial/ethnic minority counseling research criticisms. Below we outline and briefly describe ten of these criticisms.

MAJOR CRITICISMS OF RACIAL/ETHNIC MINORITY FOCUSED COUNSELING RESEARCH

1. *Lack of conceptual/theoretical frameworks to guide research*

There has been some criticism that empirical studies in the field are fragmented, arising more out of curiosity than a formal conceptual or theoretical foundation which would appropriately guide and direct the research. Without a solid conceptual/theoretical base to guide hypotheses, research efforts are likely to be nonsystematic, resulting in a disparate mix of contradictory findings.

2. *Overemphasis on simplistic counselor/client process variables and a disregard for important psychosocial variables within and outside the culture that might impact counseling*

The concern here is that too much research has focused on simple, that is easily measurable, process variables such as clients' preference for the race of the counselor, client expectations about counseling, and general client attitudes toward counseling. Little research, the critics note, has been devoted to important psycho-social variables which may be more difficult to study, but which are vital to understanding the role of counseling with American minority groups. Some of these latter variables include learning styles, communication patterns, social practices, and the cumulative effects of discrimination, oppression, and poverty.

3. *Overreliance on experimental analogue research*

Concern has been expressed that a majority of multicultural research has used analogue designs whereby the subject pools have consisted of pseudo-clients (e.g., students) and pseudo-counselors (e.g., graduate students in counseling) instead of "real" clients and counselors. The major concern with this form of research is that the results will have limited generalizability to actual client and counselor populations.

4. *Disregard for within-group or intracultural differences*

Research has had the tendency to compare minority groups against the White majority group as if the latter were the standard for comparison, the group to be emulated. This research emphasis has resulted in the portrayal of diverse minority groups as homogeneous. In other terms, the high degree of heterogeneity existing within minority populations has been glossed over, thus further reinforcing ethnic stereotypes and categorizations.

5. *The use of easily accessible college student populations*

Many researchers are academicians employed in universities. They have ready access to the university population and as a result frequently use college students, particularly undergraduates, as samples in research studies. However, questions can be raised about how representative college student samples are to the larger community. Thus, the results of university-based research that relies on minority college student samples may have limited generalizability to the larger minority community.

6. *Reliance on culturally encapsulated psychometric instrumentation*

Multicultural counseling researchers have had the tendency to employ instrumentation that was developed by and for the White middle-class culture. There is great concern that the blanket use of White-normed instruments with culturally-different clientele is misleading and inappropriate.

7. *Failure to adequately describe one's sample in terms of socioeconomic status (SES)*

Critics argue that researchers have been sloppy in conducting and reporting their research. One major concern deals with authors not adequately describing their sample. Socioeconomic status (SES) of the research subjects is one characteristic that is particularly important to understanding the sample. A number of authors have noted that there probably are more differences between varying SES groups than between racial/ethnic groups.

8. *Failure to delineate the study's limitations*

Multicultural scholars have been critical of authors who do not openly acknowledge the limitations of their research in the *Results* and *Discussion* sections. Researchers have a professional obligation to evaluate their study's limitations, particularly with regard to the generalizability of their results to populations outside their subject pool.

9. *Lack of adequate sample sizes*

Some authors have noted that many of the studies reported in the published research have relied on small, geographically-bound samples. Concern has been raised that the readers of such studies may overgeneralize the results to the whole minority population under investigation.

10. *Overreliance on paper-and-pencil outcome measures*

Research in racial/ethnic minority counseling has relied too heavily on paper-and-pencil instruments as outcome measures. The relevance of subjects' written responses to real world behavior is questioned. A call has been made to incorporate more observable behavioral measures as dependent variables in multicultural studies.

ARE THESE CRITICISMS JUSTIFIED? A SYSTEMATIC RESPONSE

Ponterotto (1988b) noted that many criticisms leveled at the current status of multicultural research have stemmed from authors writing in a reflective way about their personal views on the topic. He noted that little attention had been given to systematically examining published studies to establish a valid data base within which these criticisms could be verified or nullified. In his recent study, Ponterotto (1988b) examined all the racial/ethnic minority-focused research published in the counseling psychology profession's most respected research journal—the *Journal of Counseling Psychology*—to see which of the most common research criticisms were justified. He found that a number of the criticisms and concerns were in fact warranted, but that others were not.

This chapter extends and broadens the Ponterotto (1988b) investigation and systematically examines the methodologies employed in recent multicultural studies published in a number of counseling journals. Ponterotto (1988b) examined one journal over an eleven-year period; we will focus on a recent six-year period across five nationally refereed counseling journals.

Method

Identifying Leading Counseling Journals

Heath, Neimeyer, and Pedersen (1988) recently conducted a Delphi Poll on the future of cross-cultural counseling. In their polling of 53 identified experts in the field, a number of important areas were covered, including the identification of major national journals most likely to publish multicultural counseling research studies. The highest ranked journals were, in order: *Journal of Counseling Psychology, Journal of Counseling and Development, Journal of Multicultural Counseling and Development, Journal of Cross-Cultural Psychology,* and *The Counseling Psychologist.* Four of these journals are specifically counseling-focused; only the *Journal of Cross-Cultural Psychology* is not a counseling journal, it is a psychology journal. For this chapter we have decided to review the four *counseling-specific* journals delineated above. Also, we have added the major national mental health counseling journal to our list — the *Journal of Mental Health Counseling*.

In summary, the five journals to be systematically reviewed are:

1. *Journal of Counseling Psychology (JCP)*

JCP is published quarterly by the American Psychological Association.

2. *Journal of Counseling and Development (JCD)*

JCD is published six times per year by the American Association for Counseling and Development.

3. *Journal of Multicultural Counseling and Development (JMCD)*

JMCD is the quarterly journal of the Association for Multicultural Counseling and Development (AMCD), a division of (and published by) the American Association for Counseling and Development.

4. *The Counseling Psychologist (TCP)*

TCP is the journal of the Division of Counseling Psychology (Division Number 17) of the American Psychological Association. This quarterly journal is published by Sage Publications.

5. *Journal of Mental Health Counseling (JMHC)*

JMHC is the quarterly journal of the Association for Mental Health Counselors (AMHC), a division of the American Association for Counseling and Development. *JMHC* is published by Sage Publications.

Journal Review Procedure

Each issue of these five journals was reviewed over the six-year inclusive period 1983 to 1988. All articles with a focus on *North American racial/ethnic minority groups* (but not other minority groups such as women, the elderly, the handicapped, or internationals [e.g., foreign students]) was identified and classified as either an empirical study (i.e., data based) or a conceptual article (i.e., not data based). The empirical studies were further examined to identify whether they used quantitative or qualitative research methods. Table X details the number of conceptual, empirical, and total article counts for the five journals over the six-year period of inquiry.

Table X reveals that over the six-year inclusive period, 1,800 articles were published in the five journals. Of this aggregate total, 184 (or 10.2%) focused on North American racial/ethnic minority groups. It is also evident in Table X that of the 184 minority articles, 93 were conceptual articles and 91 were empirically-focused. Of this latter total, 80 used

Table X.
Racial/Ethnic Minority Focused Articles in Five
National Counseling Journals, 1983 to 1988

Year	Total Articles	# Minority Articles	% Minority Articles	# Quant. Articles	# Qual. Articles	# Concep. Articles
Journal of Counseling Psychology (JCP)						
1983	87	7	8.0	6	0	1
1984	66	6	9.1	6	0	0
1985	75	3	4.0	3	0	0
1986	72	6	8.3	5	0	1
1987	63	3	4.8	3	0	0
1988	64	7	10.9	6	1	0
Total	427	32	7.5	29	1	2
Journal of Counseling and Development (JCD)						
1983	154	6	3.9	1	0	5
1984	147	5	3.4	1	1	3
1985	159	3	1.9	0	0	3
1986	156	11	7.1	3	2	6
1987	123	5	4.1	0	0	5
1988	149	10	6.7	1	2	7
Total	888	40	4.5	6	5	29
Journal of Multicultural Counseling and Development (JMCD)						
1983	20	20	100.0	10	0	10
1984	9	9	100.0	7	0	2
1985	19	18	94.7	8	0	10
1986	20	20	100.0	10	2	8
1987	16	14	87.5	7	0	7
1988	17	13	76.5	3	2	8
Total	101	94	93.1	45	4	45
The Counseling Psychologist (TCP)						
1983	44	1	2.3	0	0	1
1984	45	2	4.4	0	0	2
1985	43	11[a]	25.6	0	1	10
1986	37	1[b]	2.7	0	0	1
1987	39	1	2.6	0	0	1
1988	44	1	2.3	0	0	1
Total	252	17	6.7	0	1	16

Table X. Continued

Year	Total Articles	# Minority Articles	% Minority Articles	# Quant. Articles	# Qual. Articles	# Concep. Articles
Journal of Mental Health Counseling (JMHC)						
1983	22	0	0.0	0	0	0
1984	16	0	0.0	0	0	0
1985	18	0	0.0	0	0	0
1986	27	1	3.7	0	0	1
1987	24	0	0.0	0	0	0
1988	25	0	0.0	0	0	0
Total	132	1	0.8	0	0	1
Grand Total	1,800	184	10.2	80	11	93

[a]This was a special issue of *The Counseling Psychologist* on cross-cultural counseling (edited by Smith & Vasquez, 1985).
[b]This review article by Atkinson and Schein (1986) focused on counselor-client similarity in counseling and devoted one specific section to racial similarity research.

quantitative research methods, and 11 used qualitative methodologies. (Quantitative and qualitative research methods are discussed at length in Chapters Eight and Nine.)

As the criticisms outlined earlier were in regard to quantitatively-based research, and given that the majority (87.9%) of all the data-based articles were of this type, our systematic critique will focus exclusively on these 80 studies.

Results of Systematic Review

General Characteristics of the Studies

The first points of interest in regard to these 80 studies are in reference to which racial/ethnic minority groups are being studied, and where in the United States these studies are being conducted. Tables XI and XII summarize this data.

Table XI indicates that Black only samples were the most frequently studied minority group (36.3%), followed by studies in which Whites were compared to Blacks (15.0%). Other racial/ethnic groups or comparative groupings receiving moderate attention were Hispanics (7.5%), American Indians (7.5%), three different groups studied simultaneously (7.5%), and four racial/ethnic groups studied concurrently (7.5%). These data

Table XI.
Racial/Ethnic Breakdown of Samples from 80 Quantitative Articles
Appearing in Five National Journals

Racial/Ethnic Group	Frequency	Percentage of Total N (80)
Blacks Only	29	36.3
Blacks and Whites	12	15.0
Hispanics Only	6	7.5
American Indians Only	6	7.5
Three Groups	6	7.5
Four Groups	6	7.5
Hispanics and Whites	5	6.3
Asian Americans Only	4	5.0
Whites Only	2	2.5
Asian Americans and Whites	2	2.5
Blacks and Hispanics	1	1.3
Asian Indian Americans	1	1.3
Total	80	100

indicate that all four major racial/ethnic groupings are receiving some research attention. However, with regards to specific racial/ethnic groups studied, Black samples far outnumber the other three minority groups. It would be fair to say that given the changing demographics in the United States (particularly with regards to Hispanics; refer back to Chapters One and Three) more research attention is needed in the area of counseling Hispanics, Asian Americans, and American Indians.

It is also interesting to note where a majority of the multicultural research is being conducted. Assessing geographical locales of studies is important because different regions of the country vary in value systems and even in conceptions of "normal" and "abnormal" behavior (see discussions by Pedersen, 1988; Ponterotto, Alexander, and Hinkston, 1988). One must be cautious, for example, in generalizing the results of research done in the Deep South to samples in the Northeast and West Coast.

Table XII outlines where minority counseling research has been conducted during the past six years. The data indicate that all major regions of the U.S. are represented. A collective majority of the studies were conducted in the Midwest (18.8%), West (13.8%), Southeast (12.5%), and Northeast (11.3%). Unfortunately, in 16.3 percent of the studies reviewed the authors neglected to specify the region where the investigation was conducted.

Table XII.
Geographic Breakdown of Sample Locales

Region	Number of Studies	Percentage
Midwest	15	18.8
West	11	13.8
Southwest	10	12.5
Northeast	9	11.3
Southwest	7	8.8
Two or More Regions	6	7.5
Canada	5	6.3
South	3	3.8
Hawaii	1	1.3
Not Specified	13	16.3
Total	80	100

METHODOLOGICAL CRITICISMS: A REASSESSMENT

Earlier in this chapter ten major research criticisms often cited in the multicultural literature were briefly outlined. It was also highlighted that the validity of these criticisms had yet to be objectively examined (with exception of Ponterotto's [1988b] work exclusively with the *Journal of Counseling Psychology*). Now we turn to these criticisms once again, this time, however, we examine them against an extensive 80-study data base encompassing five national journals over a recent six-year period.

Criticism One: *Lack of Conceptual/Theoretical Framework to Guide Research*

The Introduction section of each article was examined for specific theoretical and conceptual underpinnings in counseling/psychological theory. Twenty-eight studies (35.0%) clearly developed their research hypotheses according to established theory in one of five areas: vocational (or career) development (15.0%), personality development (11.3%), social influence (3.8%), social learning (2.5%), and psychosocial development (2.5%). Table XIII summarizes this data.

A number of researchers in multicultural counseling, including Casas (1984, 1985a), Ponterotto and Benesch (1988), and D.W. Sue (1978) have noted that a majority of research in the field is not solidly grounded in counseling theory. Thus many studies are conducted without a conceptual framework to adequately guide potentially important research questions and hypotheses. Certainly, one important characteristic of meaningful

Table XIII.
Specified Conceptual/Theoretical Bases for Quantitative Studies

Theory	Number	Percentage
Vocational/Career Development	12	15.0
Personality and Racial		
Identity Theory	9	11.3
Social Influence Theory	3	3.8
Social Learning Theory	2	2.5
Psychosocial Development	2	2.5
No Theory Specified	52	65.0
Total	80	100

and fruitful research is that it systematically and carefully tests particular hypotheses that would be predicated in a conceptual/theoretical model (see Osipow, 1983). The result of theoretically driven research is that the findings serve to validate or disprove various theoretical tenets, which in turn allow one to assess either strengths of or needed modifications in the theory.

On the other hand, the potential result of nonconceptually-based research is that no theory is being systematically advanced and tested, resulting in the collection of disjointed and unrelated findings. In this instance, research studies purporting to study the same or a similar topic result in fragmented and contradictory findings. In speaking on this topic with regards to all the multicultural research published in the *Journal of Counseling Psychology* over the last eleven years, Ponterotto (1988b) provides a specific example:

> . . . most of the research on counselor-client racial similarity is tied to the fact that minorities tend to underutilize counseling or terminate from it prematurely. One plausible explanation for this fact, the reasoning goes, is that there aren't enough minority counselors, who would really be preferred by prospective minority clientele. Researchers then use this line of reasoning to examine racial preferences in minority clients. Although a very interesting topic, it has not been firmly grounded in a guiding conceptual/theoretical model, and as a result, one-half or so of the studies point to racial preferences, and about one-half or so do not (p. 414).

In our systematic review, only 35 percent of the studies published in five of the profession's most prestigious national journals were well-grounded in counseling/psychological theory. It appears that the strong criticisms of Casas (1984, 1985a), D.W. Sue (1978) and others are warranted in this area. Later on in this chapter we provide specific conceptual and methodological considerations for racial/ethnic minority research.

Criticism Two: *Overemphasis on Simplistic Counselor/Client Process Variables and a Disregard for Important Psych-Social Variables Within and Outside the Culture that Impact Counseling*

The major topical focus of each quantitative-based study was identified. Table XIV rank orders the most frequent topics of study. The four most investigated topics were: counselor-client racial similarity and counseling process (12.5%), vocational/career counseling issues (10.0%), academic and educational counseling issues (10.0%), and assertiveness topics (7.5%).

Table XIV.
Ten Most Frequent Topical Foci of Studies

Topic	Number	Percentage
Counselor-client racial similarity and counseling process	10	12.5
Vocational/career choices/aspirations	8	10.0
Academic/educational issues	8	10.0
Assertiveness	6	7.5
Client preferences for counselor race	5	6.3
General attitudes toward counseling	4	5.0
Client needs assessment	4	5.0
Scale validation	4	5.0
Self-concept/self-esteem issues	3	3.8
Effectiveness of counseling interventions	3	3.8
Combined "other" topics	25	31.3
Total	80	100

Table XIV reveals that quite a number of important areas are being studied by multicultural researchers. As Casas (1984, 1985a) anticipated, however, a number of essential topics need to receive greater attention in the quantitative research. Among them are communication styles in minority groups, socializing practices, learning styles, and the effects of discrimination and poverty. It also appears that more studies on the acculturation process and its relation to mental health are warranted. These important variables give shape and meaning to the minority client's (and counselor's) behavior in the counseling context (see Casas, 1984, 1985a; Lonner & Sundberg, 1985; Ponterotto, 1988b). Later on in this chapter, and in Chapters Eight and Nine, the reader will be provided with pragmatic guidelines for conducting research on these important variables.

Criticism Three: *Overreliance on Experimental Analogue Research*

Research in multicultural counseling has been classified into three major methodological design groupings: *analogue* research, *survey* research, and *archival* research (Atkinson, 1983, 1985).

In *analogue* studies, the researcher attempts to closely simulate some aspect of "true" counseling while at the same time maintaining maximum control over experimental manipulations. In analogue research, subjects are usually pseudo-clients (e.g., college students), or pseudo-counselors (e.g., graduate students in counselor training programs) who are randomly assigned to various experimental levels of some stimulus situation (see Atkinson, 1983; Gelso, 1979). A good example of an experimental analogue study examined in our review is that by Pomales, Claiborn, and LaFromboise (1986). In this investigation, 54 Black students (not "real" clients) were randomly assigned to one of four treatment conditions in which they viewed a videotape of a mock counseling session. Each of the videotapes varied by counselor (one of two females) and the counselor's manipulated level of "cultural sensitivity." The subjects then rated the videotaped counselor on the Cross-Cultural Competency Scale (Hernandez & LaFromboise, 1985) and the Counselor Rating Form (Barak & LaCrosse, 1975).

Survey research involves giving subjects a written survey or questionnaire on some aspect of counseling. Recent multicultural survey research has examined clients' or prospective clients' perceived counseling needs, attitudes towards counselors and counseling, preferences for counselor race, and satisfaction with counseling. An example of a recent survey research report is that conducted by Atkinson, Furlong, and Poston (1986). These authors sampled 128 Black community college students' preferences for various counselor characteristics. The particular counselor characteristics included ethnicity, age, education, attitudes and values, personality, sex, socioeconomic status, and religion.

Archival research involves going back over client records in counseling agencies to determine if relationships exist between certain counselor and client variables and select aspects of counseling process and outcome. Recent archival research has focused on differential effects of counseling treatment, differential counseling duration rates, and racial comparisons of presenting symptomologies. Tracey, Leong, and Glidden (1986) used an archival research design to examine the records of 3,050 past college counseling center clients for the purpose of determining the relationship between client race and presenting concerns.

In addition to analogue, survey, and archival designs, racial/ethnic minority research can take on the form of a *"true experimental"* study. In the "true" experiment, investigators use actual clients and practicing counselors, and they randomly assign client subjects to controlled levels of "real" treatment. This type study is usually conducted in the natural counseling setting, such as in a community mental health clinic or college counseling center. An interesting example of a true experiment taken from our review is that by Neimeyer, Fukuyama, Bingham, Hall, and Mussenden (1986). In this study, 20 volunteer counselor-trainees were randomly assigned to one of two specific cross-cultural training exercises (based on Pedersen's [1988] Triad Model of training). The counselor trainees' practice sessions were videotaped and then evaluated by trained raters who completed the Counselor Rating Form (LaCrosse & Barak, 1976) and the Global Rating Scale (Gazda, Asburry, Balzea, Childers, & Walters, 1977). Each counselor also completed two self-assessment reports measuring competency and performance comfort (see Neimeyer et al., 1986).

In our review of the 80 identified empirical studies, the overwhelming majority (72.5%) were *survey* in nature. Table XV presents the frequency and percentage counts across the four types of research design. *Analogue* designs were second in frequency (12.5%) followed by *true experimental* designs (8.8%), and *archival* designs (6.3%).

Table XV.
Research Designs Employed in Quantitative Studies

Design	Number	Percentage
Survey	58	72.5
Analogue	10	12.5
"True" Experiment	7	8.8
Archival	5	6.3
Total	80	100

Criticisms (e.g., Atkinson & Schein, 1986; Casas, 1984; Casas et al., 1986) noting that multicultural researchers rely too heavily on analogue studies are not supported by our data base. Only 12.5 percent of all studies utilized this research design. It appears that if any single research design is overused, it would be survey research, which accounted for 72.5 percent of the studies. A journal-by-journal analysis would probably reveal that some journals are more inclined to publish analogue studies (e.g., 44.4 percent of all racial/ethnic minority focused articles published in the *Journal of Counseling Psychology* from 1976 to 1986 used analogue methods [Ponterotto, 1988b]), but viewed collectively, this research methodology is not overused.

Criticism Four: *Disregard for Within-Group or Intra-Cultural Differences*

Each of the quantitatively-based studies was examined to see whether authors considered within-group or intracultural differences in their minority samples. Of the 80 studies, 27 (33.8%) incorporated within-group differences into their designs.

A number of authors, including Atkinson (1983, 1985), Casas et al. (1986) and S. Sue et al. (1985), have expressed concern that by comparing one ethnic group to another, each becomes perceived as homogeneous. Such a comparison serves to hide the heterogeneity existing in racial/ethnic groups. In fact, it is possible that interethnic group comparisons do more to perpetuate ethnic categorizations and stereotypes than they do to prevent them (Campbell, 1967; S. Sue et al., 1985).

Given that less than one-third of the studies we reviewed examined differences within ethnic groups, we have to conclude that this major criticism is indeed justified. Certainly authors need to consider examining within-group differences in their multicultural work. Good examples of research that has effectively conceptualized and tested within-group differences include the Parham and Helms (1985b) study with Blacks, the Sanchez and Atkinson (1983) study with Mexican Americans, and the S. Sue and Zane (1985) study with Chinese Americans. Later on in this chapter, we identify important within-group differences to be studied among racial/ethnic groups.

Criticism Five: *The Use of Easily Accessible College Student Populations*

Table XVI presents a breakdown of the population from which study samples were taken. As is clearly evident from the Table, undergraduate college students were by far the most studied group (46.3%). High school students were the next most frequently studied population (17.5%), followed by general community residents (8.8%), and combined undergraduate and graduate student samples (5.0%).

Casas and others (Atkinson & Schein, 1986; Casas, 1984, 1985a; Casas et al., 1986) have been quite concerned that a majority of the cross-cultural research published in the profession's most respected national journals

Table XVI.
Populations Studied in Quantitative Investigations

Population	Number	Percentage
College Undergraduates	37	46.3
High school students	14	17.5
Community residents (General population)	7	8.8
Undergraduate *and* graduate students	4	5.0
Elementary school students	3	3.8
Community college students	3	3.8
Undergraduate *and* community college students	3	3.8
Mental health clinic outpatients	2	2.5
Graduate students	2	2.5
Professional counselors	1	1.3
Multicultural counseling experts	1	1.3
Nurses *and* professional counselors	1	1.3
Graduate students *and* professors	1	1.3
Adolescents	1	1.3
Total	80	100

relies too heavily on student samples. His concern is that consumers of this research may generalize the results of student-based research to their nonstudent counterparts in the community. Counseling issues of minority students on the college campus, particularly on the predominantly White campus, may not be reflective of the larger minority community. Based on our accumulated six-year data base, the Casas concern is warranted, and researchers are encouraged to extend their research programs beyond the "ivory towers" of the campus.

Criticism Six: *Reliance on Culturally-Encapsulated Psychometric Instrumentation*

An examination of the 80 studies revealed that only 25 (31.3%) incorporated counseling instruments that were developed specifically for use with minority populations. The interpretive dangers of using instruments developed for the White middle class with culturally-different groups are many, and are discussed elsewhere in the literature (e.g., Lonner & Ibrahim, 1989; Pedersen, 1988; Ponterotto, 1988b; D.W. Sue, 1989) as well as in Chapter Eight of this book. The lack of adequate minority-based instrumentation is one of the greatest limitations of the 80 studies reviewed here.

More research attention must be directed towards developing instruments that are meaningful and relevant to racial/ethnic minority groups. Fortunately, recent literature has begun to validate and incorporate such instruments, a sampling of which include: the Racial Identity Attitude Scale (Helms, 1990; Parham & Helms, 1981, 1985a, 1985b; Ponterotto & Wise, 1987), the Cultural Mistrust Inventory (Terrell & Terrell, 1984), and the Cross-Cultural Counseling Inventory (Pomales et al., 1986). Chapter Eight presents a comprehensive review of a number of instruments with great potential for use in racial/ethnic focused counseling research.

Criticism Seven: *Failure to Adequately Describe One's Sample in Terms of Socioeconomic Status (SES)*

Twenty-eight (35.0%) of the 80 studies reported the sample's SES. Given that writers have repeatedly stressed the importance of acknowledging the SES of minority samples (e.g., Casas, 1984, 1985b; Ponterotto, 1988b), it is unfortunate that only a small percentage of authors attended to this issue in their sample description sections. Ponterotto (1988b), in reviewing the multicultural research published in the *Journal of Counseling Psychology* over the last decade, speculated on why authors may neglect to specify sample SES:

> ... many of the samples were university based and researchers may take the SES status (e.g., middle class) of the sample for granted; or they, perhaps, may not think SES status relevant to understanding the sample. Given that individual minority students at universities can be quite heterogeneous with regards to family and personal income, it appears that an adequate SES description of the sample is usually warranted (p. 414).

Criticism Eight: *Failure to Delineate the Study's Limitations*

Concern has been expressed that counseling studies in general (Scherman & Doan, 1985), and racial/ethnic minority counseling studies in particular (Ponterotto, 1988b) have not adequately addressed and highlighted their generalizability limitations. In our review, 49 of the 80 studies (61.3%) discussed the limitations of their research in regards to methodological procedures and result generalizability. This important aspect of research reporting was one of the stronger characteristics of this collective group of empirical studies. It appears that criticisms in this area are not fully justified, although it would be ideal if 100 percent of the studies acknowledged for their readers the limitations of their study.

Criticism Nine: *Lack of Adequate Sample Sizes*

Casas (1984, 1985a, 1985b) has criticized the recent multicultural literature on grounds that its samples are small and not generalizable to the larger minority community. We examined the sample sizes of each of the 80 quantitative studies, and we noted whether the focus of the investigation was on one specific ethnic group or on two or more ethnic groups. Table XVII presents the results of this examination.

Table XVII.
Sample Sizes of Studies Focusing on One or
Two or More Racial/Ethnic Groups

Sample Size	One Ethnic Group		Two or More Ethnic Groups	
	Number	%	Number	%
n < 100	17	21.5	14	17.7
100 < n < 200	21	26.6	9	11.4
200 < n < 300	5	6.3	1	1.3
300 < n < 500	1	1.3	2	2.5
n > 700	2	2.5	7	8.9
Total	46	58.2	33	41.8

Note: Total N = 79 because one study did not specify sample size.

Twenty-one and one-half percent of the studies focusing on one specific racial/ethnic group, and 17.7 percent of the studies examining two or more groups had sample sizes of 100 or less. Twenty-six point six percent of the studies examining one ethnic group, and 11.4 percent of studies looking at two or more groups had sample sizes from 100 to 200. The remaining sample size breakdowns are listed in Table XVII.

It is somewhat difficult to respond to the Casas sample size criticisms because sample size appropriateness is contingent on the research design incorporated. For survey research (the most common form of research used in our group of studies [72.5%]) and archival research larger sample sizes are usually more appropriate. In this respect, with 39.2 percent of all studies incorporating sample sizes of 100 or less, and 38.0 percent using sample sizes between 100 and 200, the Casas criticism is justified. However, with regard to true experiments and experimental analogue studies where subjects are randomly assigned to manipulated levels of an experimental treatment or stimulus, the Casas criticism is not as relevant.
Criticism Ten: *Overreliance on Paper-and-Pencil Measures as Dependent Variables*

Ponterotto (1988b) notes that a detriment to the pragmatic validity of minority-focused counseling research has been an overreliance on paper-and-pencil outcome measures (e.g., counselor rating scales, counseling attitude surveys, self-disclosure questionnaires, and assertiveness inventories). We reviewed each of the 80 studies to examine what percentage incorporated observable, behavioral outcome measures. Only 8 (10.0%) of the studies used outcome measures other than traditional paper-and-pencil instruments. Examples of studies incorporating behavioral outcome measures include Folensbee, Draguns, and Danish (1986), Huey and Rank (1984), and D. Sue, Ino, and D.M. Sue (1983). This latter study highlights the importance of incorporating behavioral outcome measures into the designs of studies. The authors (D. Sue et al., 1983) demonstrated that although Asian American subjects had lower assertiveness scores on paper-and-pencil measures, they were as assertive as whites on actual behavioral (i.e., acting in an assertive manner) measures of performance.

DISCUSSION

This chapter has identified ten major racial/ethnic minority counseling research criticisms and has proceeded to examine the validity of these criticisms against a systematically accumulated data base of 80 empirical studies. The results show that a number of these major criticisms are indeed justified, and also, that a few have not been supported by the data. In summary, of the ten criticisms, our view is that six were fully supported, two were partially supported, and two were unfounded. Below we specify the criticisms accordingly.

Six Numbered Criticisms Supported by the Data

1. Lack of conceptual/theoretical frameworks to guide research.
4. Disregard for within-group or intracultural differences.
5. The use of easily accessible college student populations.
6. Reliance on culturally encapsulated psychometric instrumentation.
7. Failure to adequately describe one's sample in terms of socioeconomic status (SES).
10. Overreliance on paper-and-pencil measures as dependent variables.

Two Numbered Criticisms Only Partially Supported by the Data

2. Overemphasis on simplistic counselor/client process variables and a disregard for important psychosocial variables within and outside the culture that might impact counseling.
9. Lack of adequate sample sizes.

Two Numbered Criticisms Disputed by the Data

3. Overreliance on experimental analogue research.
8. Failure to delineate study's limitations.

CONCEPTUAL AND METHODOLOGICAL RECOMMENDATIONS

Based on our review and validation of these ten criticisms, the remaining sections of this chapter will delineate specific conceptual and methodological suggestions for consideration in future racial/ethnic group focused counseling research.

Conceptual Considerations

A majority of the research we reviewed in this chapter was not solidly grounded in counseling/psychological theory. For example, the most popular topic studied was counselor-client racial similarity and counseling process (refer back to Table XIV). As noted earlier, this research emphasis stemmed from the question of whether minority clients would prefer to see and work with minority counselors. Most of the studies examining this topic lacked a theoretical framework within which research questions could be conceptually linked. In reading many of the studies, it seemed the idea for the investigation arose mainly out of a researcher's curiosity.

The results of counselor preference studies are quite mixed (see reviews by Atkinson, 1983, 1985), with some studies reporting a similar race preference and others not. We suggest that researchers use conceptual/theoretical models to guide their investigations. The results of such investigations could then be fed back into the conceptual model in an attempt to improve, update, and/or modify the theory.

Returning to the topic of client preferences for counselor race, researchers must first ask what it is about society, the environment, and social interaction that would make race a salient variable in counseling. Ponterotto (1988b) recently suggested that this research could be grounded in theories of oppression (D.W. Sue, 1978), or in theories of racial identity development for both minorities (e.g., Cross, 1971; Helms, 1984; Parham, 1989) and the white majority culture (Helms, 1984; Ponterotto,

1988a; Sabnani, Ponterotto, & Borodovsky, in press). Ponterotto (1988b) states that:

By following conceptual models in their investigations, researchers will be able to expand their questions of preference for whom? or preference for what? to include: how helper preferences develop? who develops strong preferences and who does not? under what socio-environmental conditions does prefer- ence matter? and how does honoring client preferences for a helper relate to counseling effectiveness? (see also Gordon & Grantham, 1979) (p. 415).

In the last ten years a number of conceptual models for multicultural counseling practice (e.g., Benesch & Ponterotto, 1989; Casas & Vasquez, 1989; Casas, Vasquez, Barón, & Ponterotto, 1991; Helms, 1984, 1990; Parham, 1989; Ponterotto & Benesch, 1988; D.W. Sue, 1978; S. Sue & Zane, 1987) and training (Carney & Kahn, 1984; Rowe 1988; Sabnani, Ponterotto, & Borodovski, in press) have appeared. At this time little research has been directed at testing and validating these models. Research in these areas is needed and would contribute greatly to our understand- ing of the complex dynamics and process of multicultural counseling.

Methodological Considerations

In this section, five specific areas worthy of consideration in the methodological design of future racial/ethnic minority counseling research are delineated (see also Ponterotto, 1988b, 1989).

1. Culture is not an easy topic to study. It is a complex phenomena with a multitude of interceding and interacting factors and components (see Pedersen, 1988). To effectively and comprehensively study culture, a variety of research methods probably should be incorporated. Our review revealed that the majority of empirical research in the area has been quantitative in nature. Although these methods, whereby groups are compared with one another through collective mean differences, are valuable and provide reliable inferential (inferring to the sampled popu- lation as a whole) information, not all counseling research questions can be answered in this manner. We strongly believe that it would behoove counseling researchers to embrace qualitative research methods that have been effectively employed in the related disciplines of ethnology, cultural anthropology, and sociology (see Helms, 1989a; Ponterotto, 1988b).

As counseling researchers broaden their methodologies, an expansion of statistical techniques used to analyze and present data will occur. Such qualitative research methods as ethnographic reports, field techniques, oral histories, intensive interviews, and N = 1 studies could provide valuable observational information to the cross-cultural researcher that could not be acquired through traditional quantitative research methods. The more research methodologies employed to examine a single counseling question, the more enlightened researchers will become as to the dynamics and processes involved in the particular research query (see also, Zimmer, 1976). Fortunately, in very recent years, alternative research methods have begun to gain increased attention and credibility in the counseling psychology literature (see major contribution by Hoshmand, 1989).

Examples of qualitative research in multicultural counseling extracted directly from the present six-year review of studies include the following:

A) The Inouye and Pedersen (1985) content analysis of ethnic programming presented at annual conferences of the American Psychological Association.

B) Ross's (1984) cross-cultural comparison of adult development among Anglo- and Mexican-Americans using tape-recorded interview procedures.

C) The Marme and Retish (1988) case study of a Vietnamese refugee family.

D) Brandell's (1988) clinical case study of treatment issues in counseling the biracial child.

E) The Foster and Seltzer (1986) naturalistic investigation which incorporated an intensive case study analysis of "personal excellence" in the face of urban poverty.

F) McKenzie's (1986) ethnographic field observations of West-Indian American clients.

G) The Reisman and Banuelos (1984) study which utilized personal interviews to examine career fantasies in the barrio.

H) Ponterotto's (1986) content analysis of all the conceptual and empirical articles published in the *Journal of Multicultural Counseling and Development* over a recent five-year period.

I) Ponterotto's (1988b) eleven-year content analysis of the empirical studies published in the *Journal of Counseling Psychology*.

J) The Smith and McMillon (1986) intensive program description (case study) examining the efficacy of counselors as educational facilitators.

These ten studies represent a sampling of the qualitative research appearing in recent racial/ethnic minority-focused counseling research.

Chapter Nine is devoted exclusively to an expanded discussion of qualitative research methods.

2. It is important that multicultural researchers refrain from the use of conceptualizations that tend to compare minority groups to Whites as if the White majority group was the "normal" standard (see Pedersen, 1988; Ponterotto, 1988b). Certainly, at times, examining between group or intercultural differences is important and provides valuable information to the counselor. However, if this research focus is employed, then researchers should avoid attributing negative valences to the identified differences (see Casas, 1984, 1985a).

It is suggested that researchers consider incorporating within-group (or intracultural) conceptualizations into their designs. For example, instead of examining whether Mexican Americans have less or more favorable attitudes towards counseling services than do Anglos, researchers might examine what aspects or variables within the Mexican American culture differentiate between those who have favorable attitudes and those who do not. Does one's level of acculturation into the dominant majority culture, for example, predicate certain attitudes toward counseling? Examining attitudes in this framework highlights the great heterogeneity existing in the Mexican American culture, and importantly, serves to prevent journal readers from overgeneralizing and stereotyping that "all Mexican Americans" have negative [or positive] attitudes toward counseling (see work of Ponce & Atkinson, 1989; Sanchez & Atkinson, 1983).

Researchers have identified a number of variables that can be used as independent variables in within-group focused designs. Among the more frequently cited are level of acculturation (Atkinson & Gim, 1989; Atkinson, Whiteley, & Gim, 1990; Padilla & Lindholm, 1984; Ponce & Atkinson, 1989), level of racial identity development (Austin, Carter, & Vaux, 1990; Helms, 1989b, 1990; Parham & Helms, 1985a, 1985b; White & Parham, 1990; Ponterotto, 1989; Ponterotto et al., 1986), generational status (S. Sue & Zane, 1985), and SES (Ponterotto, 1988b). A note of caution should be noted in terms of SES. Gordon (1973) has expressed concern that traditional SES categories used with the majority culture may not be appropriate for use with all racial/ethnic groups. If SES is used as a comparative variable in multicultural research, it should be categorized from a culturally-specific vantage point (Ponterotto, 1988b).

3. In recent years, "culture" has become a sensitive issue in counseling. Some argue that the counseling profession, namely the American Association for Counseling and Development (AACD) and the Division of

Counseling Psychology (Division Number 17) of the American Psychological Association (APA), does not attend fairly and adequately to minority issues in their political, administrative, and research agendas. As identified in this chapter, research in multicultural counseling has been particularly criticized. Although our view is that culture certainly is an important variable in counseling, we do believe that there is danger of "overculturalizing." Culture is not the only variable that influences human behavior and social interaction. Certain factors that all people experience and that often lead to psychological stress are important in assessing mental health status. Some of these factors include the loss of significant others, economic deprivation, serious illness, uncertainties about the future, and rapidly changing world events (Casas, 1984). Some authors have emphasized recently that cross-cultural research is needed to identify aspects of the counseling relationship and counseling process that could be said to transcend culture (Benesch & Ponterotto, 1989; Ponterotto, Alexander, & Hinkston, 1988; Ponterotto & Benesch, 1988).

4. Multicultural researchers have relied heavily on instruments designed to measure constructs conceptualized from the White middle-class perspective. Some examples include the constructs of *depression, self-concept,* and *assertiveness.* These constructs as defined and measured by White middle-class standards, have been indiscriminately used with culturally-different groups. In speaking specifically on this topic, Ponterotto (1988b) asks:

> What value is there in administering a depression rating scale to someone from a culture (e.g., some Asian cultures) that does not even conceptualize such a construct, that has no equivalent word for it in their vocabulary (see discussion by Marsella, 1980)? (p. 416).

As another example, one can examine the construct of "self-concept." Is it justified to use a self-concept scale developed for middle-class Whites with racial/ethnic minority groups? Might it not be more meaningful to define and develop a "self-concept" construct as envisioned and perceived by members of the particular ethnic group under study?

It is suggested that future multicultural research be devoted to developing culture-specific instrumentation (see also Chapter Eight). If a researcher believes that a particular construct and its concomitant measuring instrument can be generalized to a culturally-different group, then culture-specific norms should be developed before the results are interpreted (see an example of norming by Itzkowitz & Petrie, 1988).

5. In our review, we did not locate many multicultural counseling studies focused on the mental health strengths of minority cultures (see also discussions by Casas, 1984; D.W. Sue et al., 1982). Some suggested areas for research in this area include identifying the positive aspects of being bicultural, and examining positive coping strategies used by minority group individuals. D.W. Sue (1981) emphasizes the need to balance research on both the positive aspects and psychological stressors of particular racial/ethnic groups.

SUMMARY

This chapter has examined methodological issues in racial/ethnic minority focused counseling research. Ten frequently noted criticisms of methodology in such research were identified and evaluated vis-a-vis a systematic review of 80 empirical studies. Based on the aggregate data pool, six of the criticisms appeared to be fully justified, two were partially supported, and two were found to be unsubstantiated.

With an understanding of conceptual and methodological concerns related to racial/ethnic group research in hand, we now turn in Chapter Eight to a discussion of culturally-sensitive quantitative methods for counseling research. Chapter Nine will then address qualitative methods in multicultural counseling research.

Chapter Eight

QUANTITATIVE METHODOLOGY AND INSTRUMENTATION IN RACIAL/ETHNIC MINORITY COUNSELING RESEARCH[*]

Carefully designed research is important for studying any topic or group in counseling. However, given the complex and politically sensitive dynamics of inter-racial relationships in the United States (Helms, 1990; Sabnani et al., in press), and given the damage resulting from early psychological research which directly and indirectly labeled minorities as pathological, deficient, and less cultured (refer back to Chapter Five), multicultural investigators must be particularly careful and ethically vigilant (see Chapter Ten) as they design and interpret research.

Building on the contents of Chapter Seven, the present chapter (a) highlights additional considerations in designing quantitative methodologies with racial/ethnic minority groups; and (b), provides a detailed review and critique of select, culturally-specific instruments designed for use in multicultural research.

TOWARD DESIGNING MORE CULTURALLY SENSITIVE QUANTITATIVE RESEARCH

Chapter Seven noted that 85 percent of the recent quantitative research reviewed utilized either survey (72.5%) or analogue (12.5%) designs. Much less frequent were the incorporation of true experiments (8.8%) and archival (6.3%) designs which collectively accounted for only about 15 percent of the recent multicultural research in leading counseling journals. In this section we briefly highlight design factors and cultural issues related to each of these quantitative methods.

---

[*]Portions of this chapter were summarized from Sabnani, H.B., and Ponterotto, J.G. (1990). Racial/Ethnic Minority-Specific Instrumentation in Counseling Research: A Review, Critique, and Recommendations. Paper presented at the annual meeting of the American Psychological Association, August, Boston, MA.

Designing Survey Questionnaires

As indicated, survey methodology has been incorporated frequently in counseling research with racial/ethnic minority groups. Surveys are popular with researchers because they allow one to examine large samples in a relatively short period of time. Surveys and questionnaires are also particularly well suited to the study of client attitudes, counseling preferences, and stated mental health problems, topics which have received significant attention in the multicultural area.

There are many books available on designing survey research (e.g., Backstrom & Hursh, 1963); our purpose in this brief section is not to teach survey methodology but to discuss issues we believe particularly relevant when designing surveys with culturally- and economically-diverse groups. Below we highlight three factors to consider when designing survey/questionnaire research with culturally-, linguistically-, and economically-diverse populations. These factors are not meant to replace the more traditional survey validation procedures (e.g., content validity and clarity checks by "experts," as well as the standard reliability and validity considerations), but to augment such procedures. Finally, we believe that the points discussed below apply, as well, to any paper-and-pencil instrument or assessment device.

1. Surveys should be carefully tailored to the particular group under study. The language in the survey should be pretested on a pilot sample representing your eventual sample population. A pilot test will allow you to answer the following questions: Are the items measuring what you want them to measure? Is the survey wording and format (e.g., multiple choice, Likert-type) understandable and meaningful to your group? Are we certain the survey is not too long, or the print too small? Are any items potentially offensive to the projected sample group?

These are important questions to consider, because unless individuals have experience with the U.S. educational process (and some recent immigrants naturally do not) where written tests and surveys of many sorts are common, then they may not be accustomed to scale-type surveys. Even if the surveys are completed by the sample in such a case, the results may not be meaningful. Our pilot-test process usually involves administering the survey to a sample size of about 5 percent of the eventual full sample, and then interviewing the respondents to assess their perspective on the clarity, meaningfulness, and purpose of the survey.

2. An important consideration when conducting survey/questionnaire research with immigrant or indigenous groups, is whether a standard English version of the instrument needs to be translated. Effective and comparable questionnaire translation is a complex, arduous process. Fortunately there are some excellent sources available that describe in detail how to engage in this process (see Brislin, 1986). The more common and accepted methods include forms of *back translation* and *decentering*, by where one bilingual translates from the source language to the target language, and another bilingual blindly translates back to the source. This procedure is then repeated for several rounds with different bilinguals. Moving back and forth between languages facilitates a *decentering process* where no specific language is the "center" of attention (Brislin, 1970, 1986; Brislin, Lonner, & Thorndike, 1973).

Given the complexity of language, and the various culture-specific emotional components attached to certain words and phrases, it is recommended that even after a multiple-round decentering process the survey should be restandardized and normed with the target population. A basic assessment of test-retest reliability or of internal consistency reliability is not sufficient, the *validity* of the translated instrument must be reassessed (see Guthrie & Lonner, 1986).

3. Consider carefully how you plan to distribute and collect the surveys or questionnaires. Will you use a mailing or distribute the surveys yourself? Keep in mind the validity and generalizability of your findings if only a small percentage of questionnaires are returned. Some socioeconomic and cultural groups, depending on their past contacts with White middle-class establishments (e.g., government agencies, universities), may not be fully trustful of the researcher's intent. Community residents, of *any* racial/ethnic group, are probably not as cooperative as college sophomores "captured" in a classroom setting. Reasons for the possible lack of cooperation have been previously discussed in Chapter Three.

If your survey response rate and cooperation level is low, can you interpret why this is so? This could yield clinically and sociopolitically useful information. Attempt to interview a random subsample of both survey respondents and nonrespondents to assess their compliance rationales, and their general reactions to the survey. Are there characteristics (e.g., demographic, attitudinal) that distinguish your respondent group from the nonrespondent group?

Clinically Meaningful Analogue Research

In analogue research (defined in Chapter Seven), the investigator attempts to simulate the actual counseling process while maintaining experimental control over the independent and dependent variables. Some racial/ethnic minority scholars noted in the early 1980s (e.g., Casas, 1984) that counseling research relied too heavily on analogue designs. However, our more recent methodology review (see Chapter Seven) did not find an overreliance on these designs. Nonetheless, analogue designs are a mainstay of quantitative methodology in the counseling field and it is important when working with ethnically different groups to carefully consider the implications of one's design and research results.

Analogue research attempts to carefully isolate an identified counseling process or outcome variable (e.g., the counselor's level of self-disclosure) so that the precise influence of this variable, and this variable only, can be studied. Well-designed analogue research has high levels of internal validity (see Gelso, 1979).

As will be highlighted in Chapter Nine, every research design possesses inherent strengths and weaknesses. Analogue research gains internal validity at the expense of external or ecological validity. Analogue counseling designs can become so controlled that they lose their resemblance to "real" counseling. First, most analogue designs use pseudo-clients (e.g., college students) and pseudo-counselors (e.g., counseling graduate students) who volunteer to participate in the study. One can understandably question how generalizable such research is to the "real world" of counseling. Secondly, the contrived nature of the analogue interview (which is often only 10 to 15 minutes in duration), where every word and movement of the counselor is standardized and rehearsed, is inconsistent with "real" counseling which is highly interactive and complex. Third, in some analogue designs the nonequivalency of the manipulated independent variable almost assures a particular outcome. For example, if one wants to compare the relative preferences of Mexican American students for one of two videotaped counselors, one portraying a behavioral approach, and the other a client-centered approach, it must first be demonstrated that both counselors are equally effective at their respective approaches. Unfortunately, a number of studies have been published which indicate that a behavioral or structured approach (as an example) is preferred by minority subjects; but upon close examination of the analogue videotapes and/or transcripts, it becomes clear that *anyone* (of any ethnic group) watching the videotapes would have preferred the behavioral approach because it was simply better counseling.

Certainly there is a place for analogue designs in counseling research generally and racial/ethnic minority counseling research specifically (see related discussion by Claiborn, LaFromboise, & Pomales, 1986). However, given the Eurocentric bias of most counseling theories and instruments (Helms, 1989b; see also Chapter Five), the multicultural researcher needs to be particularly careful in how one interprets and generalizes from such research.

Designing True Experiments and Archival Studies

Traditional experiments and archival studies were not very common in the multicultural counseling literature reviewed systematically in Chapter Seven. Such methodologies may be more common in the clinical and psychiatric literature. As with all the quantitative designs introduced in Chapter Seven and elaborated upon here, a good design is a good design, regardless of the racial/ethnic group being studied. More important to the accuracy, utility, and benefit of multicultural research are the theories from which the questions/hypotheses are derived (see Chapter Five) and the specific topical areas addressed (see Chapter Six). If these are culturally biased (e.g., White, middle-class, male, theoretical conceptualizations; and research queries that have a "blame the victim" or "culturally-deprived" expectation) then our multiethnic knowledge base will be faulty regardless of the methodological sophistication of the research design (see Casas, 1985a; Ponterotto, 1988b).

As with the other methodologies discussed in this chapter and the next, there are numerous full-length books focusing on research design. It is not our intention in this brief section to review archival and true experimental methodologies in depth, but to highlight an aspect of these quantitative methods that we believe particularly important in the conduct of research with culturally diverse groups.

A concern with past experimental and archival research is that racial/ethnic groups were compared to one another on various psychological variables without accounting for other nonethnic differences. As a result, differences were sometimes attributed to racial differences, where very likely the differential findings could have been the result of socioeconomic, educational, geographic and regional, or religious differences.

As will be highlighted later in this chapter, a thorough understanding of your comparison samples in true experimental and archival designs is a must. Sampling in such designs usually follows a form of randomization; and we advocate a matched random sampling procedure (a process discussed in all research design textbooks). This is not always done in multicultural counseling research. Comparison samples selected for an archival or experimental design should be matched on as many variables as possible—age grouping, socioeconomic status, and educational level are examples of demographic matching variables. Depending on the topic under study, the researcher may need to match samples on extraneous psychological variables. To illustrate this point, a recent study that characterizes a well-controlled archival study is here presented.

Johnson and Brems (1990) examined the presence of racial bias in the Minnesota Multiphasic Personality Inventory (MMPI) with an inpatient psychiatric population. MMPI profiles of 22 Black and 22 White patients were systematically matched on four different variables: gender, identical age, Axis I Diagnosis, and Axis II Diagnosis. The authors found that when Black and White patients were carefully matched on these variables, no statistically or clinically significant differences between the two samples emerged. This study is important because it provides evidence that race-based differences in MMPI profiles found in past studies may have been due more to these moderating variables than to race per se. The study also provides evidence that the MMPI may be appropriate for use with Black patients without the need for separate norm development. However, as Johnson and Brems (1990) appropriately caution, their study was limited in sample size and geographic regional spread. Clearly, much more research in this area is needed before we can ascertain the true multicultural potential and applicability of the MMPI. Nevertheless, the Johnson and Brems (1990) study demonstrates how moderating variables need to be carefully matched in archival research.

Further Considerations in Quantitative Research

In addition to the above considerations posited for specific methodologies, there are a number of general research issues that also merit attention in any quantitative studies focusing on culturally-diverse populations. Below we profile three such issues.

1. Take special care in documenting demographic characteristics of the sample. Knowing simply the ethnic make-up and mean age of one's sample is insufficient in assessing result generalizability. Describe the sample fully: mean and median age; educational level (and in immigrant groups, where the education was received); socioeconomic status; gender; preferred language and level of acculturation (see next section) in immigrant samples; the level of racial identity development; geographic region of the study, and any other sample characteristics you believe your reader should consider when interpreting your results. As a rule of thumb, the more accurately you can describe your sample, the more accurate you can be in determining the generalizability of your results.

2. One important characteristic of a good journal article or research report is that the authors take care to comprehensively and honestly discuss the limitations of their study. Every study has its limitations; and highlighting these limitations serves to provide readers and future researchers with important directions and needed methodological modifications for subsequent research.

3. Any paper-and-pencil instrument is naturally limited for a number of reasons: (a) one never knows for sure (even with adequate pilot testing) that the respondent is interpreting and understanding the items in the manner the researcher expects; (b) the researcher can seldom control for the many variables that may influence a subject's response set, for instance mood, alertness, need to answer as expected and other social desirability factors; and (c) even the respondent answering items honestly may not have a good depth of self-understanding when considering affective (i.e., how do you feel about . . .) and cognitive (i.e., what do you think about . . .) item stimuli, and therefore may be responding honestly but not accurately.

These limitations apply to any subject group and to any paper-and-pencil instrument, whether it be a survey questionnaire, a standardized attitude scale, or an objective personality test. Given that most extant instruments used in multicultural counseling research were developed for and normed on White middle-class persons, many of these limitations become magnified vis-a-vis racial/ethnic minority group research. As will be highlighted in the next section of this chapter, there is a strong need to devote more research attention to the development of racial/ethnic minority-specific instrumentation. There are a number of such instruments with good potential for research and these are critically reviewed in the remainder of this chapter.

If researchers believe that an originally White-normed instrument may be applicable to culturally and socioeconomically diverse groups, then the researchers should develop their own norms with subsequent samples, and should also reestablish the psychometric properties of the scale. Psychometric indeces such as reliability, validity, and basic factor structures should be established for each new sample. Further, we advocate that researchers consider linking their quantitative, paper-and-pencil data with the results of more qualitative phenomenological research. We specify such procedures in Chapter Nine.

CULTURE-SPECIFIC INSTRUMENTATION IN RACIAL/ETHNIC MINORITY COUNSELING RESEARCH

Chapter Seven highlighted the fact that only 25 percent of the empirical research reviewed from 1983 to 1988 utilized instruments specifically developed for use with culturally-diverse populations. There is a clear need to devote increased research attention to the development and validation of instruments conceptualized from a racial/ethnic minority perspective (Ponterotto, 1988b; Sabnani & Ponterotto, 1990; D.W. Sue, 1989). Further there is a strong need to identify and carefully evaluate extant instruments developed specifically for psychological research on racial/ethnic minority groups.

In this section six minority-specific instruments that can serve as valuable tools for the counseling researcher are reviewed. These instruments were selected after an exhaustive review of the counseling psychology literature. This group of instruments was selected because they varied in topical scope (e.g., client vs. counselor focus), covered a number of racial/ethnic groups, and had promise for multicultural research. The specifics of the selection methodology can be found in Sabnani and Ponterotto (1990), the recent source from which this chapter section is summarized.

The following selected instruments are reviewed in terms of their item development and psychometric properties: the Cultural Mistrust Inventory (Terrell & Terrell, 1981), the African Self-Consciousness Scale (Baldwin & Bell, 1985), the Cross-Cultural Counseling Inventory—Revised (LaFromboise, Coleman, & Hernandez, 1990), the Modern Racism Scale (McConahay, 1986), the Value Orientation Scale (Szapocznik, Scopetta, Arnalde, & Kurtines, 1978), and the Acculturation Rating Scale for Mexican Americans (Cuellar, Harris, & Jasso, 1980).

Cultural Mistrust Inventory

Scale Development

The Cultural Mistrust Inventory (CMI) was developed by Terrell and Terrell (1981) to measure Black peoples' mistrust of Whites and White-related organizations. Mistrust towards Whites develops as a result of exposure to racism by Whites. The CMI is a 48-item Likert-type scale, scored on a 7-point continuum (1 = Strongly Disagree, 7 = Strongly Agree). The final 48 items for the CMI were selected after a content validity check and item analysis (on responses 172 Black college males) of an original 81-item pool. There are four separate subscales of the CMI, with each subscale corresponding to one of the domains in which Black mistrust of Whites might exist: education and training, in politics and legal affairs, in business and at work, and in social and interpersonal settings.

Psychometric Properties

The intercorrelations between the four CMI scales are generally low (ranging from .11 to .23), supporting the relative independence of each subscale. Therefore, each of the subscales is measuring a unique aspect of cultural mistrust, and each could be used as a dependent variable in research. (The reader is referred to Ponterotto and Furlong, 1985, for a discussion of the importance of low subscale intercorrelation for multidimensional instruments.) The stability of the CMI is satisfactory with a test-retest reliability coefficient (using a sample of 69 students) of .86.

Convergent validity of the CMI was demonstrated (Terrell & Terrell, 1981) by the finding that research subjects who perceived themselves as frequent victims of racial discrimination (as measured by Terrell & Miller's [1980] Racial Discrimination Index) scored significantly higher on the CMI than did subjects who felt they were infrequent victims of discrimination. A recent study (Thompson, Neville, Weathers, Poston, & Atkinson, 1990) incorporating the CMI Interpersonal Relations and Education and Training subscales found a low to moderate correlation, .22 and .43, respectively, with the Racism Reaction Scale (a new scale developed by Thompson et al., 1990 for their study), indicating that the two instruments are probably measuring somewhat related but different concepts.

In summary, the content validation and item-analysis development of the CMI is satisfactory, as is the short-term test-retest stability. However, at this time there are no measures of the CMI's internal consistency, no data on its factor structure, and limited (one study) evidence for its convergent validity. Much more research is needed on the CMI, and we suggest starting with assessing the scale's Coefficient Alpha (for internal consistency), and with assessing its factor structure (using both orthogonal and oblique rotations) with large and diverse samples.

African Self-Consciousness Scale

Scale Development

The African Self-Consciousness Scale (ASCS; Baldwin & Bell, 1985) measures the degree to which one's beliefs, attitudes, and behaviors are affirming of one's African American life and cultural heritage. African self-consciousness is measured within four "competency" dimensions: awareness of one's African American identity and heritage; the acceptance of values and customs which affirm African American life; involvement in the liberation and development of African Americans; and, the opposition to racial oppression. Baldwin and Bell (1985) present six "manifest" areas in which African self-consciousness is likely to be expressed: politics, cultural activities, religion, education, family, and interpersonal relations. It is likely that differing levels of African self-consciousness among Black people account to a large degree for the variance found in psychological research within the African American community.

The 42-item ASCS was developed after five "expert" judges rated an initial pool of 130 items on how well each item reflected the African self-consciousness construct. Each item is scored on an 8-point Likert-type scale (1–2 = Strongly Disagree, 7–8 = Strongly Agree).

Psychometric Properties

Using a sample of 109 Black college students from Florida, Baldwin and Bell (1985) obtained a test-retest reliability coefficient of .90. The authors also demonstrated some content validity for the ASCS in the moderately high correlation (r = .70) found between scores on the scale and teachers' ratings of 50 Black college students on a checklist of African self-consciousness attributes. Finally, the ASCS has a degree of convergent validity as demonstrated in its moderate (r = .68) correlation (using 70 Black college students) with the Black Personality Question-naire (BPQ; Williams, 1981).

In summary the content validation of the final ASCS items seems thorough, and there are satisfactory indications of convergent validity and test-retest stability. However, as with the Cultural Mistrust Inventory, there is a strong need for measures of internal consistency and for thorough assessments of the scales's factor structure with both student and nonstudent samples.

The reader should be aware that the ASCS is only one of a number of instruments measuring a form of Black consciousness or sense of racial identity. Two other scales receiving attention in the literature are the Developmental Inventory of Black Consciousness (DIBS, Milliones, 1980; see also Grace, 1984, and see Sabnani & Ponterotto, 1990 for a critical review), and the Racial Identity Attitude Scale (RIAS). The RIAS is by far the most researched and widely used racial identity scale for African Americans. The RIAS has received so much scrutiny in recent years that it would be redundant to review it again here. The reader interested in a critical review of the RIAS scales is referred to Helms (1990) and Sabnani and Ponterotto (1990). Other important references for the RIAS scale specifically, and the construct generally, are Helms (1986, 1989a, 1989b, 1989c), Helms and Parham (1990, in press), Parham (1989), Parham and Helms (1981, 1985a, 1985b), Cross (1971, 1978, 1987, 1989), Hall, Cross, & Freedle (1972), Akbar (1989), Nobles (1989), E.J. Smith (1989), White and Parham (1990), Ponterotto (1989), and Ponterotto and Wise (1987).

Cross-Cultural Counseling Inventory — Revised

Scale Development

The Cross-Cultural Counseling Inventory-Revised (CCCI–R) is a 20-item, six-point Likert-type scale (with 1 = Strongly Disagree, 6 = Strongly Agree) which assesses the counselor's ability to work effectively with clients from diverse racial/ethnic groups. The CCCI–R, constructed by LaFromboise, Coleman, and Hernandez (1990), is a modification of the original Cross-Cultural Counseling Inventory (CCCI) developed by Hernandez and LaFromboise (1985). The CCCI was developed by converting the cross-cultural competencies outlined in the D.W. Sue et al. (1982) position paper into scale items. The CCCI–R is completed by an evaluator observing the counselor, and consistent with the D.W. Sue et al. (1982) position paper, the counselor is evaluated in three areas: cultural awareness and beliefs, cultural knowledge, and specific cross-cultural skills.

Psychometric Properties

Content validity for the CCCI–R was demonstrated by eight graduate student judges who arrived at a consensus that the scale items reflected the D.W. Sue et al. (1982) cross-cultural competencies. The kappa value of .59, reflected a moderate inter-rater reliability among these judges. Further inter-rater reliability (r = .84) was demonstrated among three expert judges rating 12 videotaped counseling vignettes. The CCCI–R also appears internally consistent, with coefficient alpha levels reaching .88, .92. and .95 across undergraduate students, graduate students, and faculty (see LaFromboise et al., 1990; Pomales et al., 1986).

The CCCI–R has demonstrated criterion validity in the finding that students who are perceived as more culturally competent by their clinical supervisors do in fact score higher on the scale when scored by independent judges (LaFromboise et al., 1990). Discriminant validity was established in the finding that CCCI scores correlated minimally (.01 to .28) with the Counselor Rating Form (Barak & LaCrosse, 1975) which measures general counselor effectiveness. Further, using the original CCCI, Hernandez & Kerr (1985) found that groups exposed to cross-cultural training were rated higher on the CCCI than a control group receiving no such training.

Factor analysis studies of the CCCI–R have been mixed. Using a sample of 86 university student and faculty raters, LaFromboise et al. (1990) found a unidimensional structure underlying the scale, with a single factor (from a principal components technique) accounting for 51 percent of the scale variance. Nineteen of the 20 scale items loaded (.55 or above factor loading) on this factor. A second factor analysis was conducted by LaFromboise et al. (1990) in an attempt to isolate distinctive features of the CCCI–R. This analysis resulted in a three-factor solution accounting for 63 percent of the variance. The three factors emerging were labeled "Cross-Cultural Counseling Skill," "Sociopolitical Awareness," and "Cultural Sensitivity."

In summary, the CCCI–R has acceptable levels of internal consistency, and satisfactory measures of content, construct, criterion-related, and discriminant validity. However, at this time there is no evidence of the scale's test-retest reliability. The CCCI–R is the first instrument of its kind, and it is beginning to receive the empirical scrutiny that it needs. We expect the CCCI–R to become a leading instrument in cross-cultural counseling research and training.

The reader should note that at present two new multifactor, multi-item competency scales are under validation: The Multicultural Counseling Inventory (Sodowsky & Taffe, 1990; Sodowsky, Taffe, & Gutkin, 1990), and the Multicultural Counseling Awareness Scale: From A—Self Assessment (Ponterotto, Sanchez, & Magids, 1990).

Modern Racism Scale

Scale Development

The Modern Racism Scale (MRS; McConahay, 1986), a modified version of the Old Fashioned Racism Scale (OFRS; Greely & Sheatsley, 1971), is designed to measure White peoples' racial attitudes towards Blacks. The MRS consists of six or seven items (depending on the target population), and has both a 4-point and 5-point Likert-type format.

McConahay and Hough (1976, p. 38) define modern racism as "the expression in terms of abstract ideological symbols and symbolic behaviors of the feeling that Blacks are violating cherished values and making illegitimate demands for changes in the racial *status quo*, with the person holding these beliefs also believing that discrimination no longer exists." Sabnani and Ponterotto (1990, p. 12) present an example of a MRS item: "Over the past few years, the government and news media have shown more respect to Blacks than they deserve."

Psychometric Properties

The MRS has demonstrated satisfactory internal consistency with coefficient alphas ranging from .75 to .86 across a number of large samples (utilizing between 700 and 900 adult White subjects). Test-retest stability figures for the MRS are also fairly high, ranging from .72 to .93 across various samples (see McConahay, 1982, 1983, 1986).

Construct validity for the MRS was demonstrated by McConahay (1986) in his finding that behavioral inconsistency in simulated hiring decisions by White college students was related to higher levels of prejudice as measured by the MRS. Convergent validity was demonstrated in the negative correlation (−.30) between scores on the MRS and the Sympathetic Identification with the Underdog scale (Schuman & Harding,

1963; see McConahay & Hough, 1976). Additionally, higher scores on the MRS were predictive of high levels of anti-Black feeling as measured by Campbell's (1971) Feeling Thermometer.

In summary, the MRS has satisfactory test-retest stability, and moderate to high internal consistency. There is some evidence for the construct and convergent validity of the scale. A particular strength of the MRS is its brevity, making it very easy to administer and score.

Value Orientation Scale

Scale Development

The Value Orientation Scale (VOS) was developed by Szapocznik, Scopetta, Arnalde, & Kurtines (1978) as part of a process to establish a therapeutic model appropriate to the cultural characteristics of the Cuban American population. Szapocznik et al. (1978) utilized Kluckholn and Strodtbeck's (1961) theory of world views as a foundation for identifying cultural differences between the Cuban American and other U.S. populations.

Kluckholn and Strodtbeck (1961) assume that there are variations in the way that different cultures respond to five human problems. These problems deal with how people see the nature of human beings; the relationship of humans to their environment; the preferred activity level of people; preferred time orientations; and the relationship of people to others (see also Ibrahim & Kahn, 1987, who developed the Scale to Assess World Views).

In developing the VOS, Szapocznik et al. (1978) constructed 22 items worded as problem situations, with three potential responses rated for each problem. Thus there is a grand total of 66 variables constituting the scale (see Szapocznik et al., 1978; and Sabnani & Ponterotto, 1990 for more details on the VOS).

Psychometric Properties

Moderate factorial support was found for the VOS. Four distinct factors emerged (not five as would be predicted by the Kluckholn & Strodtbeck, 1961 model; see Sabnani & Ponterotto, 1990 for psychometric details). Coefficient alphas for these factor-analytic-derived subscales ranged from .72 to .89 with a multiethnic adult population (N = 325; Mean age = 25 years), and from .46 to .76 for 208 Cuban (27%) and

Anglo-American (73%) adolescents (Mean age = 16 years). In analyzing collective responses of the samples, Szapocznik et al. (1978) found that Anglo-American and Cuban·American individuals differed significantly on a number of preferred value orientations (see Sabnani & Ponterotto, 1990).

In summary, the VOS has moderate to high internal consistency for adults, and low to moderate consistency for adolescents. There is partial support for the scale's factorial validity, but at this time there are no measures of test-retest stability or convergent validity.

Acculturation Rating Scale for Mexican-Americans

Scale Development

The Acculturation Rating Scale for Mexican Americans (ARSMA) was developed by Cuellar, Harris, and Jasso (1980) to provide a measure of acculturation for both normal and clinical Mexican-American populations. The ARSMA consists of 20 Likert-type questions where responses range from 1 (Mexican/Spanish language or culture identification, orientation, or preference) to 5 (Anglo/English orientation). Low scores indicate minimal levels of acculturation and a traditional Mexican/Hispanic identification.

The ARSMA items were generated from among the dimensions posited by Padilla and Carlos (1974) to be central to the acculturation construct: language usage, preferred ethnic interaction, ethnic identity and pride, cultural heritage, and generational proximity.

Psychometric Properties

As a measure of internal consistency reliability, Cuellar et al. (1980) found a coefficient alpha of .88 with a sample 134 Mexican American and Anglo American students and staff in training in mental health facilities. A coefficient alpha of .81 was found with 88 hospitalized Mexican Americans completing the ARSMA. A test-retest reliability coefficient of .72 was found with 16 Mexican American psychotic patients. Interrater reliabilities between two raters and between twelve raters was from moderate to high, at .89 and .83, respectively. A one-month test-retest reliability between two raters was also satisfactory, at .80 (see Cuellar et al., 1980, and Sabnani and Ponterotto, 1990 for exact significance levels of these reliability coefficients).

Content validity for the ARSMA was demonstrated through significant correlations between ratings of Mexican American patients by psychiatric facility staff and the actual ARSMA scores of the patients. Discriminant and construct validity for the ARSMA was demonstrated by generational differences in scores and by the fact that Mexicans scored lower on the scale than did Mexican Americans and Anglo-Americans (Cuellar et al., 1980).

A clear measure of the ARSMA's convergent validity was established in the significant Spearman-rank correlations with other acculturation scales: .81 with the Biculturalism Inventory (Ramirez, Cox, & Castenada, 1977); and .76 with the Behavioral Acculturation Scale (Szapocznik, Scopetta, Kurtines, & Arnalde, 1978). Finally a factor analysis with a combined sample of 222 normal and psychotic Mexican American and Anglo American participants yielded four factors, all related to the original conceptual domains posited by Padilla and Carlos (1974) as central to the measurement of acculturation.

In summary, the ARSMA is one of the more researched instruments reviewed here. Internal consistency reliability measures are from moderately high to high, and test-retest stability coefficients are from moderate to moderately high. There is generally strong support for the content, convergent, discriminat, and factorial validity of the ARSMA.

Notwithstanding the established strengths of the ARSMA, there is clearly a need for further research on the scale. For one the scale does not measure other dimensions that are assumed to be important concomitants of acculturation, for example, world views (see extensive discussion by Sabnani and Ponterotto, 1990). There is a need to study geographically-dispersed Mexican American samples. Finally, as suggested by Sabnani and Ponterotto (1990), there is the need to experimentally test the benefits of incorporating acculturation assessments into clinical diagnosis and treatment.

CONCLUSION

This chapter has highlighted some culturally-specific issues related to quantitative methodologies (i.e., survey, archival, true experimental, and archival designs) common in counseling psychology research. Again, it should be emphasized that good research design is good design regardless of the racial/ethnic group examined (see Casas, 1985a); but given the Eurocentric conceptual bias of past multicultural research (Helms, 1989a,

1989b; Ponterotto, 1988b), investigators must take special care when incorporating these designs with diverse racial/ethnic groups.

The second half of this chapter presented conceptual and psychometric reviews of six instruments specifically conceived and designed for use in racial/ethnic group research. The instruments reviewed represented a balance in terms of topical areas addressed and racial/ethnic groups covered. These reviews were summarized from Sabnani and Ponterotto (1990), and this source should be consulted for more in-depth coverage of instrumentation issues.

As highlighted in Chapter Seven, there is a need to augment traditional quantitative methods and instruments (as discussed in this chapter) with the less common qualitative methodologies. Chapter Nine now turns to an extensive discussion of qualitative research methods, and it demonstrates the use of the multimethod research approach which strategically combines quantitative and qualitative methods.

Chapter Nine

QUALITATIVE METHODOLOGY AND RACIAL/ETHNIC MINORITY COUNSELING RESEARCH

The purpose of this chapter is to highlight the value of qualitative methods to counseling research in general, and racial/ethnic minority counseling research in particular. An overview of various qualitative methods is presented and specific examples of this research in the racial/ethnic minority counseling area are posited.

THE VALUE OF QUALITATIVE METHODS TO COUNSELING RESEARCH

Clearly, for decades, quantitative methods have dominated the counseling profession in terms of graduate research training, dissertation methodologies, and published research in national journals (see Gelso, 1979; Goldman, 1976; Mathews & Paradise, 1988; Wehrly & Watson-Gegeo, 1985). In the last five or so years, however, a number of counseling psychologists have emphasized the value of qualitative methods to counselors and have bemoaned its underuse.

In January of 1989, a special issue of *The Counseling Psychologist* [*TCP*] (Hoshmand, 1989), the profession's "state-of-the-art" and leading conceptual journal, was devoted to "Alternate Research Paradigms." The publication of this special issue signaled the counseling profession's acceptance of nontraditional, nonquantitative research approaches as equally viable investigative methods in counseling psychology research. One of the contributors to this special issue was Leo Goldman, one of the profession's strongest critics of traditional quantitative methods (see Goldman, 1976, 1977, 1978). In his 1989 *TCP* contribution, Goldman states:

the traditional, reductionistic, quantity-oriented research approaches are often discordant with the practice of counseling. We all know this and see it reflected in the anxiety with which most graduate students of counseling and counseling psychology face their statistics and research courses, the heavy drudgery of

119

the dissertation, and their relief at having that over with so that they may now do work that is meaningful to them (p. 81).

Other strong supporters of qualitative research methods for counselors include Mathews and Paradise (1988). They note that mental health counselors, by the very nature of their training and experience, are skilled observers and interviewers, thus making them ideal candidates to conduct qualitative research. Ponterotto (1988b, 1989) and Helms (1989b) have highlighted the particular value of qualitative methods to racial/ethnic minority counseling research. Ponterotto (1988b) notes that given the complexity of "culture" (see Pedersen, 1988), particularly as it interacts with counseling processes, researchers should incorporate both quantitative and qualitative methodologies to study a single research question. Given the fact that both research methodologies have inherent strengths and weaknesses, parallel findings across methodologies would markedly support the convergent validity of the results (see related comments by Zimmer, 1976).

The strategy of combining multiple research methodologies simultaneously, or in a coordinated sequence, is gaining increasing popularity in the social sciences. A classic and highly readable primer on "Multi-method Research" is provided by Brewer and Hunter (1989); and Fielding and Fielding (1986) provide another important contribution explicating how qualitative and quantitative data can be linked in a coordinated sequence. Looking specifically at ethnic research, Schofield and Anderson (1987) have demonstrated how quantitative data analysis procedures could be incorporated into qualitative designs to enhance the study of children's ethnic socialization.

QUALITATIVE METHODOLOGY: AN OVERVIEW

The cornerstone of qualitative research is its *descriptive* nature. Taylor and Bogdan (1984) comment that:

qualitative methodology refers in the broadest sense to research that produces descriptive data: people's own written or spoken words and observable behavior (p. 5).

Qualitative data has often been described as "rich" in its description of people, places, habits, customs, and events.

Qualitative methodology has its roots in what philosophers and sociologists call *phenomenology* (Deutscher, 1973; Husserl, 1913). The phenomenologist attempts to understand social phenomena from the subject's personal perspective (Bogdan & Biklen, 1982; Taylor & Bogdan, 1984). The phenomenological approach stands in contrast to the *positivist* tradition (Comte, 1896; Durkheim, 1938, 1951) that forms the foundation for quantitative research. Positivists seek the facts or causes of social phenomena *separate* from the subjective experiencing of the individuals. Taylor and Bogdan (1984) summarize succinctly the distinction between the positivist and phenomenological approaches:

> Adopting a natural science model of research, the positivist searches for causes through methods such as questionnaires, inventories, and demography that produce data amenable to statistical analysis. The phenomenologist seeks understanding through qualitative methods such as participant observation, in-depth interviewing, and others that yield descriptive data. In contrast to a natural science approach, the phenomenologist strives for what Max Weber called *verstehen*, understanding on a personal level the motives and beliefs behind people's actions (p. 2).

Research procedures falling under the rubric of qualitative methodology can often be traced to the fields of anthropology and sociology where "fieldwork" was an essential investigative tool (Mathews & Paradise, 1988). The early work of Boas (1911) and Malinowski (1932) is often credited for establishing fieldwork as an important and legitimate anthropological endeavor. For more on the history and origins of qualitative methodology, the reader is referred to the excellent overviews by Bogdan and Biklen (1982) and Taylor & Bogdan (1984).

Borrowing, integrating, and extending upon the work of Bogdan and Biklen (1982) and Taylor and Bogdan (1984), below we outline four important characteristics of qualitative research and note the contrast with traditional quantitative methodology.

Four Characteristics of Qualitative Methodology

1. Qualitative Research Is Inductive

The qualitative researcher begins with initial behavioral observations and data collection from which tentative hypotheses are built or *induced*. The researcher moves from the specifics (actual filed observations) to the more general (questions and tentative hypotheses). Tentative hypotheses are then tested through further observation and data collection. At this point, more solidified, data-influenced hypotheses can be posited.

Quantitative research, on the other hand, is *deductive* in nature. The researcher begins with a general theory of counseling, from which very specific (and hopefully) testable hypotheses are deduced or dissected. An experimentally controlled study is designed to test various hypotheses, which are then either supported or refuted. If refuted, the original theory may then be modified to take into account the research results. Table XIX illustrates more specifically the qualitative-quantitative methodological distinction.

Table XVIII.
Comparative Conceptual Flow of Qualitative
and Quantitative Methodologies

Sequential Steps	Qualitative Research	Quantitative Research
Step 1	Topic/questions of interest	Counseling/psychological theory
Step 2	Collect and interpret initial data	Specific hypotheses generated from theory
Step 3	Develop tentative hypotheses	Data collection and analysis
Step 4	Collect and interpret additional data	Hypotheses are supported or refuted based on data
Step 5	Develop specific hypotheses	

2. The Qualitative Researcher Takes a Humanistic and Holistic Perspective

Qualitative researchers examine their subjects holistically, within their natural environment and contexts, and during their day-to-day activities. This naturalistic approach has the researcher interacting with her or his subjects in as natural and unobtrusive a manner as is possible. Taylor and Bogdan (1984, p. 6) note that they "blend into the woodwork" of the culture, group, or organization under study.

Through the qualitative study of people, we get to know them personally, attempting to experience reality from their perspective and from their personal frame of reference. Researchers attempt (as much as possible) to suspend and set aside their own beliefs, perspectives, and expectations, approaching the field study with the attitude of "everything here is new, nothing will be taken for granted, and everything is subject matter for inquiry." The qualitative researcher reminds one of a client-centered therapist, attempting to see life as does the client, to walk in his or her shoes and path, to achieve a deep level of human understanding and empathy.

This qualitative approach stands in sharp contrast to the quantitative researcher's goal of remaining aloof from the subjects' experience. Following the natural science methods of chemistry or physics, the quantitative investigator is atomistic and reductionistic in his or her attempts to isolate, study, and count specific and precise behaviors, attitudes, or what have you. This natural science approach often takes the subject out of her or his natural environment so that specific details can be isolated and studied in almost a laboratory fashion, similar to a chemist taking apart a water molecule to study the hydrogen atom more closely.

3. Qualitative Researchers are Flexible

It is essential to remember that the qualitative researcher begins his or her investigation with purposefully vague ideas or curiosities. Thus the researcher is not guided by preconceived notions and expectations, but by the subject behavior observed. This method requires the researcher to be flexible, reformulating questions and directions as the inquiry proceeds. Issues of design and instrumentation are secondary to the content of what is being observed (Mathews & Paradise, 1988).

Methodological flexibility, which is so central to the qualitative perspective, is antithetical to the quantitative view. This latter view sets an *a priori* standard for design and methods. Instruments are preselected, and instructions given to subjects are prerehearsed and seldom modified. Again, like the physicist or chemist, every step of the investigation is known beforehand so that all possible confounding variables may be controlled for, and the exact causes or influences of a phenomena can be quantified and subjected to statistical analysis.

4. Qualitative Researchers Emphasize Clinical Significance

Qualitative methods ensure a close fit between the data collected and the behavioral reality of the situation. Taylor and Bogdan (1984) comment that:

> By observing people in their everyday lives, listening to them talk about what is on their minds, and looking at the documents they produce, the qualitative researcher obtains first-hand knowledge of social life unfiltered through concepts, operational definitions, and rating scales (p. 7).

Quantitative researchers, by contrast, focus on standardized and precise measures to ensure reliability and potential replicability of results. Their investigative aim is first statistical significance, and then, upon multiple replications, clinical significance.

The quantitative emphasis on reliability has been questioned by Deutscher (1973, p. 41) who, as quoted in Taylor and Bogdan (1984, p. 7), states:

> We concentrate on consistency without much concern about whether we are right or wrong. As a consequence we may have been learning a great deal about how to pursue an incorrect course with a maximum of precision.

Naturally, both qualitative- and quantitative-focused researchers are highly concerned with the accuracy of their data. However, when studying human behavior in the "real world," it is not possible to achieve perfect reliability (Taylor & Bogdan, 1984).

THREE QUALITATIVE METHODOLOGIES

Participant Observation

Participant observation refers to field research in natural settings. In this method of research the participant observer interacts with, and becomes part of the social milieu of the subjects. The investigator attempts to "melt into" the setting so-to-speak, so that she or he can observe events, behaviors, and interactions as they naturally occur. The participant observer attempts to study a group or process in as natural and unobtrusive a manner as possible.

The qualitative researcher enters the field setting with a general methodology to follow and some general research interests. However, until the setting is actually entered, and the investigator becomes part of that setting, the specific research questions are not known. The researcher's procedures and research questions evolve as the study progresses.

Selecting and Gaining Entrance to a Setting

Participant observation research is hard work; it is difficult, challenging, and time-consuming. Taylor and Bogdan (1984) summarize the process well:

> The ideal research setting is one in which the observer obtains easy access, establishes immediate rapport with informants, and gathers data directly related to the research interests. Such settings seldom exist. Getting into a setting is

usually hard work. It requires diligence and patience. The researcher must negotiate access, gradually win trust, and slowly collect data that only sometimes fit his or her interests. It is not uncommon for researchers to "spin their wheels" for weeks, even months, trying to break into a setting (p. 19).

A key to successful participant observation is studying naturally-occurring phenomena. If you are perceived as an "outsider" by the group, agency, community, or whatever the setting may be, people may be guarded and not behave in their natural and normal manner. Thus, when breaking into a setting, researchers should inform the gatekeepers (those controlling access to the research setting [e.g., the principal of a high school, the president of a community organization, the warden of a prison, the leader of a street gang]) that the research will not disrupt the setting and that only nondisruptive and nonobtrusive measurements will be involved. Researchers should also guarantee confidentiality and privacy to the group under study. It should be clarified that any field notes taken will not contain names or identifying information.

Once the researcher has gained access to the setting, she or he should take care not to disrupt the natural flow of events. Invariably, researchers feel uncomfortable their first few days in the setting. It is suggested that researchers remain particularly passive throughout the initial stages of the fieldwork and focus more on getting to know the people and the setting rather than on collecting data (Taylor & Bogdan, 1984). Early on in your placement at the setting you may not want to take notes in the presence of others, and you may want to refrain from using recording devices.

Once you have gained the confidence of the setting's gatekeepers and subjects, you may become more active in asking questions and seeking specific information that you now feel is important. At this point, it may be appropriate to use recording devices. Taylor and Bogdan (1984) devote considerable attention to the issues we briefly introduced here; we strongly recommend that their book be examined closely.

Cross-Cultural and Gender Considerations in Fieldwork

Race and gender may have a powerful impact on how subjects respond to the participant observer. For instance, in his study of Black street corner men, Liebow (1967), a White man, noted

> In my opinion, this brute fact of color, as they understood it in their experience and I understood in mine, irrevocably and absolutely relegated me to the status of outsider (cited in Taylor & Bogdan, 1984, p. 43).

Gender differences can also provide additional challenges to gaining access and acceptance into a setting. Consider male researchers studying life inside a female prison, or women attempting to study day-to-day life in a male correctional facility. Likewise, women researchers studying men's behavior and interaction patterns in the context of an athletic team (or vice versa) poses additional challenges to the research process. Although this gender interaction may itself be a worthwhile topic to study, we could not expect subjects to behave in their normal manner, at least not before a lengthy adjustment period.

In-Depth Interviewing

In-depth interviewing is another mainstay of the qualitative approach. Taylor and Bogdan (1984) clarify how in-depth interviewing differs from participant observation:

> Whereas participant observers conduct their studies in "natural" field situations, interviewers conduct theirs in situations specifically arranged for the purpose of the research. The participant observer gains first-hand experience of the social world. The interviewer relies exclusively on second-hand accounts from others (p. 78).

Participant observation is not always a feasible approach to research inquiry. For example, there are some settings that an outside observer simply will not be allowed access to. Secondly, one cannot go back in time to study past events. Finally, participant observation may take months just to locate settings, negotiate visits, and get to know the subjects and settings well enough to begin to assemble valid descriptive data. On the other hand, studies based on interview procedures can usually be completed in a shorter time frame (see Taylor & Bogdan, 1984). Therefore, in a number of cases qualitative interviewing may be the most feasible methodological option.

Interview Formats

It is important to distinguish between three types of interviews: *structured, semistructured,* and *unstructured.* In *structured* interviews, the interviewer follows a standardized format, with each interviewee being asked the same questions in the same manner to enhance the comparability of findings. In structured interviewing the interviewer is simply the data collector—and the interview schedule or protocol is the research tool. Highly structured interviews, because of their rigid nature, and because of the interviewer's *lack of interpersonal involvement* in the process, is more of a quantitative research method. In this section we will focus on unstructured and semistructured interviews, both of which we consider qualitative in nature.

Unstructured and Semistructured Interviews

A hallmark of qualitative interviewing in both unstructured and semistructured formats is getting to know the interviewees well enough to capture their perceptions of the interview topic. Qualitative interviews will be successful to the point that subjects can talk freely about their experiences and their personal interpretations of these experiences. In-depth interviews are modeled around a normal conversation, where the participants become more and more comfortable with one another as the interview proceeds.

Unstructured Interviews. In unstructured interviews much of the focus and depth of the conversation is up to the interviewee. The interviewer has a general idea of the topic to be discussed, but the tone and focus of the interview is up to the subject. In unstructured interviews the researcher has not predetermined how many subjects will be interviewed or how many sessions or hours will be spent with each interviewee. As in participant observation, the specific methodology evolves as the researcher gets more involved in the process. Taylor and Bogdan (1984) note that interviewing projects take anywhere from several sessions to over 25 sessions. Depending on circumstances, a single interview may extend from under an hour to many hours in the same sitting.

Given the potential time involvement of in-depth, unstructured interviews, this method is particularly useful to studying a smaller number of subjects in great depth. If a researcher is interested more in a broader perspective than a focused in-depth understanding, then the semistructured interview procedure may be the method of choice.

Semistructured Interviews. Although researchers will vary in their approach to semistructured interviews, generally they are intended to be fairly in-depth, yet shorter and more structured than the fully unstructured interview. Semistructured interviews are ideal when the researcher is interested in a broad range of persons, situations, or settings. A semistructured interviewer also has a clearer sense of the specific subtopics to be covered in the interview. It is important to remember, however, that as a qualitative procedure, the researcher still wants to get to know the interviewee well enough so that the interview resembles an honestly self-disclosing conversation. Again, the interviewee's experiences, opinions, and interpretations are very important.

Semistructured interviews are very appropriate for the investigator with time constraints (see Bogdan & Biklen, 1982). In this case, the researcher may have a general idea of approximately how many subjects will need to be interviewed, and the approximate time she or he would like the interview to last. Based on previous research and experiences, the semistructured interviewer may also predetermine that certain subtopics will be probed in each interview. For example, instead of using unstructured, untimed interviews to study with great depth the work experiences of three or four elementary school principals, the semistructured interviewer may desire to interview around fifteen principals, each for two hours, and will cover in each interview the principals' work interactions with teachers, students, parents, other principals and the superintendent, the school board, and the media. Although both the unstructured interviews with the three or four principals and the semistructured interviews with fifteen principals may each take about 30 hours of the researcher's time, the information garnered from each procedure may vary quite markedly.

Whether the interviewer decides on the fully unstructured or semistructured procedure will depend on his/her perceptions of what kind of information would be most enlightening. Another consideration will be time constraints: In the semistructured interview procedure, the researcher has more control over approximately how much time it will take to complete the study.

A final consideration in deciding between structured and semistructured interviews is the current *state-of-the-art* knowledge in the field. For instance, in the hypothetical "principal study" described above, if not much was known about the principal's work experience, one might first consider the unstructured, very in-depth interviews with a few principals in an attempt to capture and describe salient experiences. As a result of the unstructured interviews, the researcher may find that *interactive experiences* with key constituents (e.g., teachers, students, parents, etc.) constitute a salient aspect of the job. Now, using semistructured interviews with a larger number of principals, the researcher could focus more on describing these salient interactive phenomena.

Conducting Unstructured and Semistructured Interviews

Important considerations in conducting qualitative interviews include selecting the sample, knowing when the interview portion of the study is complete, using an interview guide, and tape-recording of interviews.

Sample Selection. In most cases, when selecting participants for the interview process, the qualitative researcher is flexible, considering alternate options for soliciting interviews. Taylor and Bogdan (1984) discuss the procedure known as *snowballing,* by where initial interviewees suggest other possible participants and so forth. Once the researcher has a sense of who is to be sampled, she or he can solicit recommendations from colleagues, agencies, and a host of other sources.

The Sample Size. Normally, the number of subjects to be interviewed is not "set in stone" prior to the interview process; particularly in the case of unstructured interviews. In semistructured interviews the researcher may have a clearer sense of approximately how many subjects will be needed, particularly given external time constraints; yet in most cases flexibility is one cornerstone of any qualitative research procedure. Importantly, the actual number of cases is not nearly as significant as the potential of each case to add to the researcher's understanding of the phenomena under study (see Taylor & Bogdan, 1984).

Theoretical sampling is a term often associated with qualitative interviewing. As long as new cases continue to add valuable insights to understanding the subject matter, the researcher continues to interview. At the point that new interview cases cease to add meaningful information to the questions under study then the *theoretical saturation* point is reached and the interview process is terminated.

The Interview Guide and Recording Devices

We suggest using a general interview guide for semistructured interviews. Such an interview guide may list a number of topics that the interviewer will want to probe with each subject. It must be emphasized that the guide is not intended to be a structured protocol as in controlled question-by-question quantitative interviewing. It is important that the semistructured interviewer use her or his judgement in deciding how and when to ask probes related to the interview guide.

The interview guide is helpful when a team of interviewers is working on a research project. In such instances, the team can be assured that each of its members is probing similar areas. Then, as is consistent with the flexible qualitative method, the interview guide can be modified to include additional areas as the team meets periodically to discuss emerging themes. Thus, as with participant observation, and unstructured interviews, the methodology is always evolving as the study proceeds.

Recording devices such as tape recorders and video cameras can serve as valuable adjuncts to the interview process. Although in participant observation, where the researcher "becomes part of the setting," we often recommend against the use of recording devices, in interviewing we are inclined to use them ourselves. Unlike participant observation, which is a naturalistic study, interviewing, by its very nature is somewhat contrived. The subjects have already given their verbal and signed consent to participate as "imparters of information," thus in most cases they do not object to being tape recorded. Video recordings may create heightened anxiety in subjects, particularly in the early minutes of interviewing; however, even in this case we have found interview subjects willing to participate. The key here is carefully and honestly explaining to the subjects how the recordings will help capture the subject's perceptions during the data reduction and analysis process. (If subjects feel particularly uneasy about being recorded, or if they simply state their preference not to be recorded after the rationale for such is presented, then we turn off the recorder. More on the ethics of research, particularly as it applies to racial/ethnic minority groups, is presented in Chapter Ten.)

In our experience, tape recordings are helpful when going back over interviews and verifying your initial impressions during the interview. Also, in writing up qualitative research results, it is common to include brief quotes of select subjects. In this case, recordings become essential.

Although tape recordings may assist the qualitative researcher, we want to emphasize that the interviewer's perceptions, impressions, and experiences *during the interview* are of paramount importance. Thus it is recommended that the interviewer take notes during and/or immediately after the interview to capture her or his experiential involvement in the process. Audio recordings seldom capture the power and significance of the interview, particularly if listened to days or weeks after the occurrence.

Life Histories and Case Studies

A third category of qualitative methodology includes oral histories, life histories, and intensive case studies. Taylor and Bogdan (1984) note that in the life history or sociological autobiography, the researcher attempts to understand and present the significant experiences in a person's life along with that individual's perceptions and interpretations of these experiences. Unlike the traditional popular autobiography, a life historian actively solicits the subject's experiences and opinions and carefully constructs an accurate individual history that is consistent with external reports (e.g., records, information provided by others in a position to know about the subject).

Procedures for conducting a life history usually involve unstructured, in-depth interviews. Oftentimes these interviews are very lengthy and are stretched out over a period of a number of months to over a year. Taylor and Bogdan (1984) review the work of Klockars (1974, 1977) who prepared a life history of a professional fence. Klockars' work involved weekly or biweekly meetings with the subject over a time span of 15 months. Many life historians supplement their in-depth interviews with written narratives provided by the subject. Therefore, in addition to verbal conversations, the researcher will use the subject's written accounts, diaries, logs, and other personal documents as a source of information and discussion.

Single and Multiple Case Studies in Counseling

The aim of the case study is to provide a comprehensive and in-depth understanding of a singular counseling case. Marme and Retish (1988) note that the case study approach helps organize social data in a manner that preserves the unitary character of the individual being studied. They further note that this approach is very useful in developing further research hypotheses. Mathews and Paradise (1988) state that

> The case-study approach offers a unique opportunity for investigating the counselor-client relationship, the counselor's techniques, and the process of change in a particular client on a session-by-session basis (Hersen & Barlow, 1976) [p. 231].

Mathews and Paradise (1988) further note that much of the theoretical base for counseling and psychotherapy stems from the individual case study. As an example, Sigmund Freud's writing is replete with case studies of individual clients.

Single-subject research is also referred to as N = 1 research. In reviewing the benefits of N = 1 research, Miller (1985) summarizes the work of

Hill, Carter, and O'Farrell (1983) and D.W. Sue (1978) and lists the following:

1. It allows more adequate description of what happens between a counselor and client.
2. Positive and negative outcomes can be understood in terms of process data.
3. Outcome measures can be tailored to the specific problems of the client.
4. It allows one to study a rare or unusual phenomena.
5. It is flexible enough to allow for novel procedures in diagnosis and treatment.
6. It can be used in evaluating the effectiveness of an intervention strategy on a single client (from Miller, 1985, p. 491).

VALIDITY CONTROL IN QUALITATIVE RESEARCH

As are quantitative researchers, qualitative investigators are concerned with the *validity* of their data. *Triangulation* is a term often associated with validity methods in qualitative designs. Although writers have discussed many different forms of triangulation, we will focus on three types in this brief section.

Taylor and Bogdan (1984) discuss triangulation in terms of "the combination of methods or sources of data in a single study" (p. 68). If a researcher receives congruent information from a variety of sources, then her or his findings exhibit increased convergent validity. For instance, in studying the stressors experienced by young school children, the researcher may not only interview the children themselves, but also teachers, parents, and older siblings. This is a form of *source* triangulation, by where the researcher seeks similar topical information from a variety of sources "in the know" about the children. If the multiple sources identify similar stressors, then the researcher has more confidence in the validity of the findings.

Paralleling source triangulation is *investigator* triangulation. In this case we have multiple interviewers (or participant observers) conducting research on the same subjects or in the same setting. If various members of the research team note similar observations, then the validity of the observations is enhanced.

Finally, the researcher should be familiar with *method* triangulation.

In this instance, the researcher incorporates related methods to study the same subjects. Thus the researcher may observe a subject in participant observation format and also interview the subject using both unstructured and structured interviews. If the results of these various qualitative methods are congruent with one-another, then again, the validity of the subject profile is enhanced.

Triangulation is an important validity concept in qualitative research. The reader is referred to Denzin (1978), Fielding and Fielding (1986), and Patton (1980) for an in-depth discussion of this concept.

LIMITATIONS OF QUALITATIVE METHODOLOGY

Like quantitative research, qualitative methodology is not exempt from limitation. Every research approach has its relative strengths and weaknesses, and the key is to know which research approach is the most appropriate at any particular point given the current state of knowledge on the topic and the questions for which answers are sought. In this brief section we review some of the more obvious limitations of participant observation, in-depth interviewing, and case study methodology.

Limitations of Participant Observation

In speaking to the limitations of participant observer methodology, Mathews and P| radise (1988) state that "Because the researcher cannot observe and record everything that transpires, decisions made about what to record may reflect unconscious biases" (p. 229). Other concerns with participant observer methodology were noted earlier and revolve around the lengthy time periods that may be involved in first gaining access to the setting, and then staying within the setting long enough so that subjects feel comfortable with your presence and begin to act in their natural manner.

A final limitation of this methodology revolves around thorny ethical issues. Participant observers are often purposely vague in describing the purpose of their study to the gatekeepers of the particular setting. Taylor and Bogdan (1984) note that

> It is unwise to give details concerning your research and the precision with which notes will be taken. If they knew how closely they were going to be watched, most people would feel self-conscious in your presence (p. 25).

Participant observers need to be careful to represent their research intentions honestly while at the same time not divulging so much that the naturalistic nature of the observation becomes impossible. Taylor and Bogdan (1984) devote extensive attention to this issue and their work is highly recommended to the interested reader (see also Bogdan & Biklen, 1982).

Limitations of In-Depth Interviewing and Case Studies

Mathews and Paradise (1988) note that some interviewees may be hesitant to disclose and discuss aberrant beliefs or behaviors during a face-to-face interview. They state that certain types of personal information can be more reliably collected through quantitative-focused anonymous questionnaires. Taylor and Bogdan (1984) note that people say and do different things in different situations. These authors caution the researcher that what a person says in an interview situation is not necessarily what the person believes or will say in a different situation. Further, a total reliance on verbal statements is naturally limiting. As a form of conversation, interviewees are subject to the same exaggerations, distortions, and misperceptions that characterize any dyadic discussion.

Finally, with regard to the case-study methodology, two important limitations are noteworthy. First, given that a case study is a comprehensive study of a single entity (for example, a client), the researcher cannot generalize her or his findings to other situations or clients. Secondly, in N = 1 research, the investigator cannot assume a direct cause-and-effect relationship between pre- and posttreatment conditions (see Miller, 1985).

SELECT SAMPLES OF
RELEVANT QUALITATIVE RESEARCH

Participant Observation Studies

An excellent example of a participant observation study is that conducted by V. Michael McKenzie and reported in the *Journal of Counseling and Development* in 1986. McKenzie's (1986) "Ethnographic Findings on West Indian-American Clients" takes an in-depth look at cultural and ethnic factors influencing the lives of nine Black, male, West Indian-American youths enrolled in a middle school in a large northeastern city. The McKenzie (1986) study was actually conducted in two parts—the first involved participant observation, and the second incorporated semistructured interviews. We limit our discussion here to the participant observation aspect of his study; in the next section we discuss his interview procedures and results.

McKenzie's (1986) participant observation (used synonymously with the terms *ethnographic* and *naturalistic*) methods are best understood in his own words:

> For 6 months, I immersed myself in the school, homes, peer groups, and neighborhoods of the original nine participants. I "shadowed" them and collected data during the day and waking hours of the evening, with an average of 40 hours devoted to each student. I noted key words and phrases during my interactions with participants, but I wrote field notes immediately after observation and participation. I sometimes used a tape recorder after obtaining permission from participants (p. 41).

In analyzing and reporting his ethnographic data, McKenzie followed the guidelines of Bogdan and Biklen (1982) which guides the researcher in the selection and synthesis of recurring themes. McKenzie (1986) reduced his massive data base into three manageable themes: family orientations, family and peer group relationships, and the personal development of the adolescents.

Semistructured Interview Studies

As a result of the participant observation portion of his study, McKenzie (1986) had developed a good understanding of cultural and ethnic factors that may be related to counseling West Indian-American adolescents. To gather more specific data regarding counseling issues with these clients, McKenzie went on to conduct semistructured interviews with his original nine subjects, an additional six students, and eleven counselors and counseling psychologists. These interviews examined students' developmental issues, their view of the utility of counseling, the typical sources of assistance considered by the students, and the knowledge and skills counselors need to work effectively with this population.

Procedurally, the interviews with the 15 students averaged two hours each; and the interviews with the mental health professionals averaged 1½ hours each. Further, all but one of the interviews with the mental health professionals were tape-recorded.

Mckenzie's (1986) final analysis of data incorporated the results of both the interviews and the participant observation information described in the last section.

Another example of a semistructured interview study was that recently conducted by Ponterotto, Yoshida, Cancelli, Mendez, and Wasilewski (1990). The authors' general interest was increasing the rate of applications from African-American and Hispanic Master's Degree level students to doctoral programs in Counseling Psychology and School Psychology. At this point in their research, the authors were interested in having prospective students look through typical application packets sent by programs (see background study of Yoshida, Cancelli, Sowinski, & Bernhardt, 1989) highlighting what they found valuable and attractive in making hypothetical decisions about which doctoral programs they would apply to and why. A major goal of this semistructured interview study was to develop a "model application packet" that would increase the likelihood of a minority student applying to the program.

These researchers used an interview guide to ensure that certain areas (identified in pilot interviews) were covered in each of the 1½ hour interviews conducted with 20 Black and Hispanic master's degree students from three universities. The authors tape-recorded each interview and analyzed the data according to recurring themes. Among the important components of an "attractive application packet" were the preparation of materials (e.g., quality of print, directions for completing forms), a personal letter to the student with a contact person specified, specific financial aid information, clear program and course descriptions, the cultural environment of the school and community, services provided at the time of graduation (e.g., career planning and placement), the specific research interests and background of the faculty, and the representation of minority students and faculty already in the program and at the university.

Case Study Investigations

Marme and Retish (1988) presented a case history of a Vietnamese refugee family settling in the midwest. A focus of the case study was on two adolescents in high school and their subsequent attempts and challenges in pursuing postsecondary education. Through individual counseling sessions and interviews with various professionals and agencies working with the adolescents, the researchers were able to "descriptively capture" the bureaucratic struggles, frustrations, and barriers confronting the students. Marme and Retish (1988) conclude that the students were effectively pushed out of school because of the system's inability to understand and meet their academic and vocational needs and desires.

Another example of an intensive case study was presented by Foster and Seltzer (1986) in their study entitled "A Portrayal of Individual Excellence in the Urban Ghetto." The researchers were addressing the question: how does a minority individual develop a sense of personal excellence in the midst of urban poverty? Foster and Seltzer (1986) studied a Black male of lower socioeconomic status living in an urban ghetto. The individual was an internationally-ranked boxer, who was observed in various capacities for about 30 hours (e.g., before, during, and after bouts). The researchers also interviewed the subject as well as cohorts (e.g., another boxer, the coach). The study lasted six months.

The results of the Foster and Seltzer (1986) study were quite revealing. They conclude that the achievement of individual excellence in the face of harsh environmental factors is the result of a complex interaction between the personal attributes of the achiever and his [in this case] social network. In the case of this talented boxer, his coach (not family) was the salient and influential social factor that, in interaction with his personal will and motivation catipulted him to success.

Individual case studies allow for the in-depth examination of the client in a sociocultural context. Although, naturally, one must be careful if attempting to generalize the results of a case study, this method of inquiry facilitates a deep understanding of the client or family under study, the social and cultural forces impacting on the client's adjustment and mental health, and helps to generate culturally-relevant and appropriate options for intervention. Two recent case studies demonstrating these advantages are the Giles (1990) study of a 9-year-old Haitian boy in the New York City public schools, and the Rosser-Hogan (1990) investigation of a 33-year-old Montagnard refugee from the central highlands of Vietnam.

CONCLUSION: THE RESEARCH PROCESS

Becoming a good qualitative or quantitative researcher involves basically three processes. First, read published studies that interest you.

Reading examples of research gives you an understanding of how the research is conducted, analyzed and integrated, and reported. Second, attempt to work with an experienced (preferably published) researcher in your methodological area of interest. If you are a graduate student, attempt to work with one of your professors. If you are experienced in quantitative methods only, then hook up with a qualitative researcher and vice versa. Finally, engage in the research fully. Once you are involved in the real process, questions and challenges will arise whereupon you can return to the literature and to experienced colleagues with a firmer grasp of the information you need.

Deciding Between Qualitative and Quantitative Approaches

As highlighted earlier in this chapter, both qualitative and quantitative approaches have their relative strengths and limitations. Selecting the appropriate methodology depends on the research questions being asked and the current state of knowledge in the field.

Oftentimes when not much is known about a particular topic, qualitative methods can be of great value in exploring the topic and raising more specific questions and hypotheses to be pursued in subsequent research. Table XVIII, presented earlier, gives the reader a sense of the order of research inquiry.

Ideally, each research topic in counseling generally, and racial/ethnic minority counseling specifically, would be studied by both methods. Each methodology raises certain limitations that the other could satisfactorily address. Thus if one topic has been studied repeatedly by qualitative methods, then a quantitative approach would probably yield very fruitful results. Similarly, if a topic is replete with quantitative investigations, then studying a particular aspect more in-depth and descriptively in qualitative fashion would probably be most beneficial. We suggest to researchers that when studying a counseling topic select multiple methodologies over time to increase both the internal and external validity of your findings.

Given most research in the racial/ethnic minority counseling research area has been quantitative in focus (see Ponterotto, 1988b, 1989), we admonish readers to launch more qualitative investigations at this point in time. In addition to the qualitative work of Bogdan and Biklen (1982) and Taylor and Bogdan (1984) that we relied on heavily in this chapter, the interested reader should also refer to: Agar (1986), Brewer and Hunter (1989), Briggs (1986), Fielding and Fielding (1986), Fine and Sandstrom (1988), Gephart (1988), Goldman (1978), Gubrium and Silverman (1989), Jaeger (1988), Kirk and Miller (1986), Lincoln and Guba (1985), Lonner and Berry (1986), Marshall and Rossman (1989), Miles and Huberman (1984), and Van Maanen (1983).

Chapter Ten

RACIAL/ETHNIC MINORITY COUNSELING RESEARCH AND PRACTICE: AN ETHICAL AND RESPONSIBLE PERSPECTIVE*

The previous chapters have placed research relative to racial/ethnic minorities within a historical perspective, reviewed the major research topics that have been addressed during the last five years, and carefully assessed the methodological and qualitative status of this research. Having accomplished this feat, it is appropriate at this time to direct attention to the need to ensure that such research is not only relative but relevant to racial/ethnic minority communities in their struggle to overcome the many psychosocial problems with which they are plagued (e.g., depression, substance abuse, family disruption, unemployment, high educational drop-out rates, and overrepresentation in correctional institutions).

These problems aside, from a professional perspective, it would be safe to say that racial/ethnic minorities have received minimal benefits from the work of psychologists (Zytowski, et al., 1988); and thus, unfortunately, the strong admonitions put forth by Gordon (1973) with respect to Blacks are still relevant today for racial/ethnic minorities in general. In a nutshell, according to Gordon (1973), "white psychology stands accused of unethical conduct in its relations with the black community ... Instead of service to black people, white psychology has been flagrantly self-serving and opportunistic" (p. 88).

Recognizing the ethical and professional responsibility to make research with racial/ethnic minorities more responsive to their needs, this chapter first provides a critical examination of the *APA Ethical Principles* and the *AACD Ethical Standards* as they explicitly relate to research relative to racial/ethnic minorities; it then explores ways to make the *Principles* and

---

*Portions of this chapter were reprinted from Casas, J.M., & Thompson, C.E. (1990). Ethical Principles and Standards: A Racial/Ethnic Minority Research Focus. *Counseling and Values.* Copyright by the American Association for Counseling and Development. Reprinted with permission.

Standards more relevant to minorities; and finally identifies ways by which researchers can translate such relevance into beneficial research outcomes for minority communities. It should be noted that this chapter is an expanded version of an article written by Casas and Thompson (in press).

PRINCIPLES AND STANDARDS: PERVASIVE SHORTCOMINGS

In recent years, as a result of varied sociopolitical and professional events (e.g., the gains of the civil rights movement, the population growth of minority groups, and the burgeoning dependence by agencies on minority clients), increasing attention has been directed to the critical examination of the *APA Ethical Principles* and the *AACD Ethical Standards* as they relate to and impact on racial/ethnic minorities (e.g., Casas, Ponterotto, & Gutierrez, 1986; Cayleff, 1986; Ibrahim & Arredondo, 1986; LaFromboise & Foster, 1989; Pedersen & Marsella, 1982; Tapp et al., 1974). The consensus of these efforts has been that the *Principles* and *Standards* fall short vis-a-vis minorities across the major professional activities that these principles were designed to govern and in particular, given the focus of this book, research.

Initial efforts to understand the causes for these shortcomings globally focused on the fact that the *Principles* and *Standards* do not adequately reflect the diversity of race, culture, economic status, or gender differences that are encountered by all psychologists. More specifically, they focused on "surface indicators" including explicit references made to minorities within the text of the *Principles* and *Standards* and/or the substantive content area in which the references appeared. For instance, with respect to references, several authors (e.g., Casas et al., 1986; Pedersen, 1986) were quick to show that references (i.e., direct mention) to racial, ethnic, national origin, and/or minority groups appear only three times in both documents. With respect to the amended *APA Principles* (American Psychological Association, 1990), this observation is still true. Relative to the revised *AACD Standards* (American Association for Counseling and Development, 1988), the number of such references has increased to four.

Relative to substantive content, these same authors note that the few references that are contained in the text appear in sections that emphasize the *prevention of harm* and not the provision of benefits when conducting research with or providing service (especially clinical evaluations) to individuals from the aforementioned groups. While acknowledging that ensuring research participants against harm is warranted in all cases and, in particular, for those who take part in socially-sensitive research (Seiber & Stanley, 1988), these authors are quick to note that given the tremendous sociopsychological problems that plague minority communities, focusing solely on the prevention of harm while ignoring the provision of benefits is no longer ethically acceptable.

Other explanations were much more interpretative in nature and bridged the gamut from the accusatory to the "excusatory." For instance, Casas et al. (1986) presented the interpretation that the shortcomings via-a-vis minorities are rooted in a general lack of professional interest in and concern for understanding and effectively serving persons from these groups. From another perspective, it has been argued that, although the *Principles* and *Standards* fail to address minority groups explicitly, they do so implicitly in so far as they were developed from a universal humanistic perspective that underscores the dignity and worth of *all* individuals, the preservation and protection of fundamental human rights and (relative to benefits) the promotion of human welfare. In a similar vein, the focus on the prevention of harm rather than the provision of benefits may be rooted in the ethnocentric belief that all persons have similar access to "psychological products" (i.e., research findings and innovative practices that are presented through both professional and mass media outlets).

More recently, efforts to explain the existing shortcomings has dramatically shifted to more pervasive, underlying and significantly influential factors that are deeply rooted in the *Principles* and *Standards* themselves. More specifically, the focus has been directed to the philosophical premises that underlie the *Principles* and *Standards* and that underscore the values that are reflected in the execution of professional activities.

PHILOSOPHICAL PREMISES: A CRITIQUE

Upon careful examination, it is apparent that the philosophical premises that underlie the *Principles* and *Standards* are very narrow in scope, reflecting solely the individually-oriented values prevalent in the majority culture, while totally failing to take into consideration the rich diversity of worldviews and values that are held by individuals who are members of non-White cultures, or who do not have the economic resources to be termed "middle class", or who are female, either White or of color (LaFromboise & Foster, 1989).

When gender differences are given serious consideration, it is apparent that the underlying premises tend to solely reflect the concepts of rules, rights, and priorities that are highly valued by men (Gilligan, 1982) while totally ignoring the concepts of caring and the maintenance of relationships that are highly valued by women (Noddings, 1984, 1986) and cultures that have an altruistic outlook towards life (e.g., African culture; Harding, 1987).

The *Principles* and *Standards* aside, the situation regarding the relevance and responsiveness of research with and for racial/ethnic minorities is further complicated because of the biased assumptions that underlie counseling and therapy (Pedersen, 1987). As covered in detail in Chapter Five, many of the basic assumptions of counseling and therapy reflect the cultural (Diaz-Guerrero, 1977), psychological, social, economic, and political (Katz, 1985) contexts of the Western Euro-American cultures in which they were developed; and, unfortunately, these dominant cultural assumptions are not universally applicable (Pedersen, 1977, 1979).

PHILOSOPHICAL PREMISES: NECESSARY CHANGES

Working to overcome the shortcomings inherent in the *Principles* and *Standards*, concerned individuals have called for a variety of changes. Relative to references, some authors are calling for a rewording of specific parts of the *Principles* (i.e., the Preamble) that can help to make the implicit more explicit throughout the total document (e.g., Pedersen & Ivey, 1987; Pedersen, 1988). With respect to content, numerous authors contend that what is needed is the explicit inclusion of cross-cultural concerns in the *Principles* and *Standards*.

While such recommended changes have merit, if implemented, they could very easily result in making the *Principles* and *Standards* a very cumbersome document that in the end might very likely fall short of stimulating the professional redirection that is needed and that can only occur if the changes are philosophically-based. More specifically, what is needed vis-a-vis racial/ethnic minority groups is the infusion of more altruistic, group/community-oriented, and action driven philosophies and worldviews into the *Principles* and *Standards*.

To this end, the psychology profession should seriously consider infusing a popular feminist approach that urges the field of psychology to take a stance in relation to the community and seeks resolution of ethical dilemmas in the context of dialogue with the community (Hillerbrand, 1987); or, in line with Ivey's (1987) suggestion, develop a more relational view of ethics where the profession moves from a discourse of power of the majority to a new form of dialectics between the professional organizations (e.g., APA) and those individuals embedded in the community (but often not in power); or more altruistically, follow LaFromboise and Foster's (1989) recommendation that the profession take steps to incorporate both a care perspective and a justice perspective into the *Principles* and *Standards* especially as they impact on and/or relate to multicultural ethical decision-making.

If the philosophical concepts inherent in the suggestions and recommendations noted above were infused and/or incorporated into the existing *Principles* and *Standards* and subsequently implemented through appropriate professional channels, the proposed changes could have tremendous impact on all major professional activities and, given the focus of this book, research in particular. Needless to say, the effect on racial/ethnic minorities would be significant.

PHILOSOPHICAL PREMISES: TANGIBLE TRANSLATIONS

Some might argue that the proposed philosophical changes are too intangible to effectively translate and implement through actions that consistently result in direct positive outcomes for research subject (i.e., racial/ethnic minorities). To counteract such arguments, the remaining section of this chapter provides brief examples and recommendations of ways that the nontangible philosophical concepts can be translated into tangible actions that result in positive research outcomes and benefits for racial/ethnic minority communities.

Altruism: It would not be very difficult for counseling researchers to demonstrate an altruistic interest in racial/ethnic minority communities. As noted above, these communities are plagued with an extensive number of psychosocial problems that merit serious research attention (e.g., substance abuse, school drop-outs, etc.). Given this situation, researchers need to move beyond what has traditionally been classified as counseling research (e.g., counselor variables, client variables, interaction of counselor and client variables, etc.) and begin to conduct pragmatic research that directly addresses the prevailing psychosocial problems (see also Smith et al., 1978). Concomitantly to addressing prevailing problems, and in line with Sue's recommendation (1981), researchers should direct their efforts to psychocultural strengths inherent in minority individuals and communities to effectively confront and overcome the tremendous problems that they have historically encountered (e.g., racism, discrimination, violence, etc.).

Along these lines, but from a methodological perspective, researchers should also move from the safety of analogue research paradigms to more challenging fieldwork studies (see Chapter Nine) that would require the researcher to interact and work with minority communities in their efforts to solve "real life" problems.

Responsibility: Though the concept of responsibility could be translated in a myriad of ways, the recommendations presented here focus on increasing research relevance with special attention directed to community involvement in the total research process.

As should be self-evident, but much too frequently ignored, individuals who conduct research in minority communities should have an accurate and sensitive understanding of the targeted community. Needless to say, without such understanding, there is a high probability that any pursuant research projects will fall short of methodological validity and/or pragmatic value. In fact, it is quite possible that research findings from such "invalid" research may have a negative impact on the respective minority community.

Given the aforementioned fact that minority communities are plagued with numerous challenges and problems, researchers should consider meeting with the targeted minority community to identify and prioritize those research projects they strongly feel merit immediate attention. Having identified the project, the researcher should then consider forming a community-based advisory committee to ensure that the project is truly reflective of the needs and reality of the community. To this end, as well as to increase community support for the research, efforts should be extended to include formal and/or informal leaders of the community on the committee.

If the researcher is seeking external funding, consideration should be given to submitting a proposal for a combined research demonstration project through a nonprofit service and community-based organization so that the overhead payments could be used to support the organization's work in the community.

For the sake of relevancy, researchers must begin to consider incorporating within-group or intragroup conceptualizations into their designs (see Chapters Seven and Eleven). Doing so would help to underscore the great heterogeneity that exists within racial/ethnic minority groups. More specifically, doing so could help to: (1) eliminate the tendency to overgeneralize research findings on a respective minority group to all assumed similar minority groups; (2) reduce the propensity to "over-culturalize" (as addressed in Chapter Seven), or the tendency to attribute all findings emanating from studies on minorities to the variable desig-nated as culture or to all global concepts like race, ethnicity, and/or nationality; and (3) dispel inaccurate and entrenched racial/ethnic minor-ity stereotypes. To help researchers along these lines, a variety of inde-pendent variables that can be controlled within groups have been identified (see Chapters Seven and Eleven).

As explained in Chapters Seven and Eight, and reinforced here from an ethical perspective, researchers *must* take care to ensure the external validity of the variables/constructs that are the major foci of the studies (i.e., locus of control, depression, etc.). To ensure such validity, Atkinson et al. (1989) and Tapp et al. (1974) suggest that the relevance of research variables can be effectively addressed through the inclusion on the research team of individuals who are the target of the research project.

From the perspective of data gathering, the procedures that are uti-lized should solely consist of those that are most appropriate and *acceptable* to the target population. For instance, as covered in Chapter Nine, certain groups may not wish to participate in studies that use obtrusive methods to collect the data (e.g., videotaping) or that require them to participate in an activity which although not harmful may be uncomfort-able (e.g., extensive probing interviews). To avoid such situations, it behooves the researchers to know the culture well. For example, in certain traditional Mexican American families it may not be appropriate to have a male research assistant personally interview a female participant. It may be inappropriate to discuss certain topics when both husband and wife are present (e.g., matters pertaining to sexuality and gender issues). Finally, parents may not want researchers to ask their children certain types of questions. It should be noted that the authors are not opposed to getting all necessary information from minority groups that can accrue to their benefit; however, such information must always be obtained in the least intrusive and the most culturally sensitive manner.

Given the unfamiliarity that many minority communities and individ-uals have vis-a-vis social science research, it is extremely important that researchers clearly state and explain the rights, obligations, and privileges that these communities are entitled to relative to this research. Tapp et al. (1974) argue that a clear agreement regarding rights, obligations, and privileges between researchers and participants should be written and, for that matter, explained in a jargon-free manner. According to these authors, an important issue that needs to be carefully attended to is the participant's right to refuse participation at *any* time.

To ensure proper and relevant interpretation of findings, the researchers should verify their interpretations of the data (e.g., causal relationships) with racial/ethnic minority individuals who may have stronger and inextricable ties to the phenomena that was studied (i.e., seek validation for interpretations or seek out other interpretations that could be just as valid).

Justice: Relative to justice, researchers should be actively involved in the recruitment and retention of racial/ethnic minority undergraduate and graduate students who can be effectively used as coresearchers or research assistants. Acting like a community-based advisory board, these students can help the researcher stay on target vis-a-vis the needs and reality of the community. Such student involvement can result not only in their developing better insights to the research process, but can also result in an increased motivation for involvement in other complimentary projects that can benefit the community. In addition, the study could be designed so that minority graduate assistants work very closely with a small group of undergraduate assistants and in so doing serve as role models and mentors for these younger students. Needless to say, given the shortage of racial/ethnic minority faculty on most campuses (Ponterotto et al., in press), the availability and positive utilization of minority students as role models or mentors is extremely important in helping and motivating minority undergraduates to successfully complete their postsecondary educational goals.

Caring: This concept can easily be translated into tangible benefits. That is to say, researchers can work to ensure that their efforts result in tangible direct, indirect, short-term, and long-term benefits to the targeted racial/ethnic minority community. Direct and immediate benefits can accrue to the community by administering and conducting research projects through existing community agencies.

Indirect and future-oriented benefits can result if research findings are subsequently used to stimulate additional research or more importantly as the basis for developing and testing innovative pilot programs in the community.

To engender greater trust in research as well as a belief that research can result in a substantive product to the community, action-oriented feedback must be provided to the community. To this end, although researchers frequently offer their participants an opportunity to learn about the results of the research firsthand (i.e., by sending the participants an abstract or summary of the research findings), this practice is usually done haphazardly (Ponterotto, 1988b); and, as a result, many communities are left with the belief that researchers promise and take but seldom deliver. In the case of minority communities, the researcher must make a concerted effort to ensure that the targeted community is not only informed of the results, but also of the potential social and political actions that can emanate from these results (e.g., counseling intervention programs for dropouts).

To this end, the researcher should make use of that medium which is most effective in delivering information to the community; suffice it to say, that in most cases this would *not* be a professional journal. Furthermore, the information should be written in a brief and jargon-free style and contain: (1) the names, titles, and addresses of the researchers; (2) the goal of the research project; (3) the methods that were employed; (4) the findings; and (5) the implications that can be drawn especially with respect to programatic development and interventions; and, (6) the persons who can be contacted for additional information.

CONCLUSION

The major focus of this book is to assist counseling researchers in their efforts to conduct methodologically sound research with racial/ethnic minorities. However, as argued in this chapter, sound research on minorities should not be the only objective of the researchers. Given the tremendous number of psychosocial problems that plague minority communities, researchers should ethically direct their efforts to conducting relevant and responsive research that can help these communities to effectively confront and eventually overcome such problems.

Working from this perspective, this chapter addressed a basic mechanism or framework that the counseling profession could use to encourage or induce its researchers to conduct relevant and responsible research with minority communities. More specifically, it critically examined the

APA Ethical Principles and the *AACD Ethical Standards* as they explicitly relate to research relative to racial/ethnic minorities. Based on this examination specific recommendations were then offered on ways to make the *Principles* and *Standards* more philosophically responsive to minorities. Finally, to counteract arguments that such philosophical changes might be too intangible to effectively bring about desired beneficial research outcomes, suggestions and examples of ways to increase the probability of attaining such outcomes were presented. Reflecting and integrating these examples and suggestions, Chapter Eleven puts forth a series of recommendations regarding future research needs and directions that if heeded can only result in relevant and positive research outcomes for racial/ethnic minority communities.

Chapter Eleven

RACIAL/ETHNIC MINORITY COUNSELING IN THE 1990S: DIRECTIONS FOR RESEARCH

In this final chapter we summarize major topics covered in this book, linking them conceptually in the form of specific suggestions for future research. The overall goal of the chapter is to set a racial/ethnic minority counseling research agenda for the 1990s.

A SUMMARY OF KEY ISSUES

To conduct experimentally-valid, culturally-sensitive, and clinically-meaningful research with racial/ethnic minority groups in the United States, the counseling student or scholar must first pause to consider some of the demographic, social, political, and methodological issues covered in our earlier chapters. Chapter One presented an overview of the current status of racial/ethnic minority counseling research and highlighted the profession's strong need for intensified research efforts in the multicultural area.

There has been and continues to be extensive confusion over appropriate terminology and definitions vis-a-vis counseling racial/ethnic minority populations. Further confusion exists with regard to accurate demographic data on the majority and racial/ethnic minority populations. Chapters Two and Three addressed these points in detail and attempted to provide researchers with accurate definitions, descriptive profiles, and demographic projections. Given the social and political overtones of these issues, researchers need to address them as they conceptualize and carry out their research investigations.

Before beginning quantitative or qualitative research, it is important to understand the past, and oftentimes still present, Eurocentric bias of traditional counseling theories and research instruments. Research questions and hypotheses stem from theories, and empirical methodology relies on diverse instrumentation; if there is bias in these areas than the results and utility of the research can be seriously called into question. Chapter Four presented a comprehensive historical overview of the psychology profession's treatment of racial/ethnic minority issues, while Chapter Five addressed the cultural bias of popular and leading counseling theories.

In deciding what areas need to be addressed in the multicultural area, it is important to first examine the topics that have been covered in past research and the methodologies used to carry out this research. Chapter Six presented a topical overview of recent racial/ethnic minority counseling research noting what has been covered and outlining a conceptual model to direct future counseling investigations. Chapters Seven through Nine outlined methodological concerns, issues, and guidelines with regard to racial/ethnic minority counseling research.

Various segments of the racial/ethnic minority community have criticized the counseling and psychology professions for their failure to address significant sociopolitical issues in their research programs. Further concerns have noted that the ethical foundations for research and practice with racial/ethnic minority populations are sorely lacking. Chapter Ten highlighted ethical and community-based concerns and cautions for the conduct of socially and politically sensitive research.

In the next and final section of this book, we provide the researcher with topical areas that we believe are meritorious of future investigation. Some of these suggestions were mentioned, in part, in previous chapters; however, our task here is to present them in an orderly and sequential format. These topics can be addressed in a doctoral thesis or dissertation format, or they may serve as the foundation for a systematic, long-term scholarly research program. However, to adequately address these questions from a nonbiased perspective, the issues presented in Chapters One through Ten must first be clearly understood.

A RESEARCH AGENDA FOR THE 1990S

Clearly, being a relatively new field within psychology, the area of racial/ethnic minority counseling is in great need of further research conducted in a systematic fashion. Below we outline and clarify twelve topical areas for further research.

1. There is a strong need for accurate epidemiological data on the incidence and prevalence of psychological problems among the various racial/ethnic groups. Huang and Gibbs (1989) emphasize that this infor-

mation is important in determining whom the psychology profession is serving and underserving. Gibbs and Huang (1989b) highlight well the relevance of accurate epidemiological data to appropriate psychological assessment and intervention among minority youth.

2. A promising area for racial/ethnic minority research revolves around minority identity models. To date, most of the research has focused on Black racial identity (e.g., Helms, 1984, 1990; Parham & Helms, 1981, 1985a, 1985b; Ponterotto et al., 1986; Ponterotto et al., 1988; Ward, 1990), though, in recent years more universal models of minority identity development have been put forth (see Atkinson, Morten, & D.W. Sue, 1989). Parallel identity research on immigrant groups (e.g., Hispanics, Asian Americans) has focused on models of acculturation (e.g., Berry & Kim, 1988; Casas, 1985a, 1985b; Ponterotto, 1987, 1988b, 1989). As highlighted in Point #7 below, one major reason why this research direction is important is because it fosters a within-group emphasis, thus portraying more accurately the heterogeneity existing among all racial/ethnic groups.

3. Much of the past research on racial/ethnic minority groups in the United States has centered on the minority individual as the focus of attention. For example, studies have assessed the mental health attitudes, needs, and preferences of minority clients; other research has focused on common pathologies found in diverse groups. Although these research areas are important and can provide valuable information to the psychology profession, they can at times foster a focus on "differences," on comparing minority groups against some established or accepted norm — that is the norm of the White middle class. Needed at this time is intensified research into the mechanisms and operations of a Eurocentric political and educational system. The following questions need to be addressed: How does institutional prejudice and racism manifest itself? How does the "glass ceiling" phenomena operate in the corporate world, in academia, and in the political arena? What interventions can be made in schools, industries, and politics to expose and alter unequal opportunity?

4. Along the lines of needed research on institutional racism and bias is a need for specific investigation into mechanisms for reversing the perpetuation of the White middle-class status quo. For instance, research in schools, at all levels, can examine the effects of prejudice prevention programs. What are the key components to combating racism and prejudice? Are experiential exercises needed? Is role reversal to be included? What balance of didactic (cognitive), experiential (affective),

and behavioral training is most effective in consciousness raising and prejudice prevention? (see Parker, 1988; Pedersen, 1988). Katz (1977) and Katz and Ivey (1977) have begun important work in the specific area of White awareness training.

5. Keeping with our focus on the White majority, continued research is needed on the investigation of White racial identity development. Work in this area is beginning to receive much needed attention, and a conceptual and empirical body of literature is now developing that can serve as a fruitful guide to prospective researchers (see Carter, 1990a, 1990b; Carter & Helms, 1990; Claney & Parker, 1989; Corvin & Wiggins, 1989; Helms & Carter, 1990; Helms, 1984, 1990; Ponterotto, 1988a; Sabnani, Ponterotto, & Borodovsky, in press).

6. Much of the past research on low-income racial/ethnic minority groups has focused on their problems—poverty, stressors, unemployment, crime—with relatively little attention directed towards their strengths. A focus on the negative in the research and in the media leaves the impression in middle-class groups that certain groups or neighborhoods are fraught with problems. Naturally, the problems outlined above need to be addressed, but so to must the strengths of minority groups. For example: How do so many low-income, minority-group members function so well in a racist and classist system? What are their coping skills and stress management skills? Learning of these minority mental health strengths will allow researchers and teachers to then immunize (so-to-speak) the youth of these and other groups.

7. One point highlighted throughout this book has been to examine the tremendous intracultural or within-group diversity existing within all racial/ethnic groups in the United States. We believe this point to be so important that we again discuss it here. A simple focus on intergroup comparisons facilitates the overgeneralization of any differences identified. Within any specific racial/ethnic group there are differences due to socioeconomic status, geographic region, religion, generational status, level of acculturation or racial/ethnic identity levels, worldviews, among others. Research focusing on particular racial/ethnic groups needs to incorporate within group differences as independent variables in the design methodologies. Instruments to accomplish this were reviewed in Chapter Eight.

8. In line with the above focus on within group differences, systematic quantitative and qualitative research is needed on the phenomena of bicultural identity development. Racial/ethnic minorities in the United

States have had to always manage and negotiate two cultures—theirs of origin and the power dominant, White middle-class system. Some racial/ethnic minorities have resolved this balancing act most effectively and have internalized or integrated their bicultural views into a healthy self-view and self-concept (see related research of Parham, 1989; and Parham & Helms, 1985a, 1985b); while other members of minority groups have felt caught between two cultures, resulting in a confused self-identity—what we call the "marginal person" phenomena where the minority individual feels caught between two worlds (see Atkinson et al., 1979). Research is needed to examine the process, variety, and effects of bicultural identity development processes. Janet Helms (1990) of the University of Maryland has, in our opinion, developed and conducted ground-breaking research in this area, and we strongly urge the reader to consult her recent book focusing on Black and White racial identity development.

9. Much of the extant research in counseling has focused on adult populations, particularly college students (refer back to Chapter Seven). More research is needed examining racial/ethnic minority youth (e.g., Esquivel & Keitel, 1990; Gibbs & Huang, 1989b), the elderly (e.g., Markides & Mindel, 1987), and the family system (e.g., Ho, 1987; McGoldrick, Pearce, & Giordano, 1982).

10. In line with focusing on the family system and family dynamics, more research is needed on primary prevention, and parent training programs. Developing a healthy self-concept begins with parental acknowledgement and positive acceptance from birth. Parents of all ethnic and cultural groups and of all social classes receive little systematic parent training. We believe this is an important area for future counseling and educational research. Casas and Furlong (1990) have begun community-focused research into the development of multilingual literature (pamphlets, comic strips, etc) aimed at lower-income Hispanic parents and focusing on parent-training vignettes.

11. There is a need for research into assessment, testing, and general instrumentation with racial/ethnic minority populations (Lonner & Ibrahim, 1989; Sabnani & Ponterotto, 1990; D.W. Sue, 1989). For decades we have relied on instruments normed primarily on the White middle class. The demographic changes taking place in the 1990s necessitate new and extensive norm sampling on both preexisting and contemporary instruments (refer back to Chapter Eight for an extensive discussion on this topic).

12. Acknowledging the complexity of cross-cultural counseling (Pedersen, 1988), we advocate research into both etic (culturally universal) and emic (culture-specific) aspects of the counseling process (see Atkinson et .al., 1989; Ponterotto & Benesch, 1988). Much more research and writing in the area of indigenous models of mental health is needed (Pedersen, 1988). Western-trained counselors have had minimal exposure to non-Western models of counseling and therapy; yet given the multicultural diversity in the United States, all mental health professionals should be knowledgeable in alternative therapies. Along with the indigenous or culture-specific modes of helping, Ponterotto and Benesch (1988) have called for increased research into helping processes that may be more likely to transcend culture. For example, research has already examined value differences between cultures, but is there a set of universally acceptable values? Virtually no research in the counseling literature has addressed this question.

Finally, in keeping with our view that culture and cross-cultural counseling are quite complex, we advocate increased interdisciplinary research in the area. Anthropologists, sociologists, psychologists, and political scientists all have their own body of multicultural research, yet seldom do students and scholars from these respective academic domains work together. We strongly urge greater interdisciplinary cooperation in the study of mental health across cultures (see also Lonner & Ibrahim, 1989; Pedersen, 1985; Ponterotto, 1989).

CONCLUSION

This chapter briefly reviewed the various topics covered in the book and then presented 12 directions for future research. Given the relative youth of the racial/ethnic minority specialization in counseling (see Heath et al., 1988), most topics already covered in past research need to be further examined with diversified research methodologies. The 12 topics we highlighted in this chapter are particularly worthy of research attention. Certainly there are other topics in the multicultural area that need systematic research inquiry, and prospective researchers of both the majority and minority groups should work collaboratively and in consultation with minority communities as they prioritize, conceptualize, and begin systematic research.

The 1990s promises to be an important decade for the United States as the projected demographic changes begin to take shape and racial/ethnic minorities move towards becoming this nation's numerical majority. The 1980s produced a number of multicultural, or cross-cultural counseling-focused books dealing with counseling issues and clinical cases, and we hope that this research-focused textbook will now stimulate much needed quantitative and qualitative work in the racial/ethnic minority counseling area.

REFERENCES

Acosta-Belen, E., & Sjostrom, B.R. (Eds.). (1988). *The Hispanic experience in the United States: Contemporary issues and perspectives.* New York: Praeger Publisher.

Agar, M.H. (1986). *Speaking of ethnography.* Qualitative Research Methods, Volume 2. Newbury Park, CA: Sage Publications.

Akbar, N. (1989). Nigrescence and identity: Some limitations. *The Counseling Psychologist, 17,* 258–263.

Allen, E.A. (1988). West Indians. In L. Comas-Diaz & E.E.H. Griffith (Eds.), *Clinical guidelines in cross-cultural mental health* (pp. 303–333). New York: John Wiley and Sons.

American Association for Counseling and Development. (1988). *Ethical Standards.* Alexandria, VA: Author.

American Council on Education (1988). *Minorities in higher education.* Seventh Annual Status Report. Washington, DC.

American Psychological Association (APA). (1981). Ethical principles of psychologists. *American Psychologist, 36,* 633–681.

American Psychological Association (APA). (1987). Resolutions approved by the national conference on graduate education in psychology. *American Psychologist, 42,* 1070–1084.

American Psychological Association (APA). (1990). Ethical principles of psychologists. Rev. ed. *American Psychologist, 45,* 390–395.

Arbona, C. (1990). Career counseling research and Hispanics: A review of the literature. *The Counseling Psychologist, 18,* 300–323.

Arlow, J.A. (1989). Psychoanalysis. In R.J. Corsini & D. Wedding (Eds.), *Current psychotherapies* (4th ed.) (pp. 19–64). Itasca, IL: Peacock Publishers.

Asamen, J.K., & Berry, G.L. (1987). Self-concept, alienation, and perceived prejudice: Implications for counseling Asian Americans. *Journal of Multicultural Counseling and Development, 15,* 146–160.

Association for Counselor Education and Supervision (ACES) Commission on Non-White Concerns. (1979). ACES position paper on non-White concerns. *Counselor Education and Supervision, 18,* 245–250.

Atkinson, D.R. (1983). Ethnic similarity in counseling psychology: A review of research. *The Counseling Psychologist, 22,* 79–92.

Atkinson, D.R. (1985). A meta-review of research on cross-cultural counseling and psychotherapy. *Journal of Multicultural Counseling and Development, 13,* 138–153.

Atkinson, D.R., Furlong, M.J., & Poston, W.C. (1986). Afro-American preferences for counselor characteristics. *Journal of Counseling Psychology, 33,* 326–330.

Atkinson, D.R., & Gim, R.H. (1989). Asian-American cultural identity and attitudes toward mental health services. *Journal of Counseling Psychology, 36,* 209–212.

Atkinson, D.R., Morten, G., & Sue, D.W. (1979). *Counseling American minorities: A cross-cultural perspective.* Dubuque, IA: William C. Brown.

Atkinson, D.R., Morten, G., & Sue, D.W. (1989). *Counseling American minorities: A cross-cultural perspective* (3rd. ed.). Dubuque, IA: William C. Brown.

Atkinson, D.R., Ponce, F.Q., & Martinez, F.M. (1984). Effects of ethnic, sex, and attitude similarity on counselor credibility. *Journal of Counseling Psychology, 31,* 588–590.

Atkinson, D.R., & Schein, S. (1986). Similarity in counseling. *The Counseling Psychologist, 14,* 319–354.

Atkinson, D.R., Winzelberg, A., & Holland, A. (1985). Ethnicity, locus of control for family planning, and pregnancy counselor credibility. *Journal of Counseling Psychology, 32,* 417–421.

Atkinson, D.R., Whiteley, S., & Gim, R.H. (1990). Asian-American acculturation and preferences for help providers. *Journal of College Student Development, 31,* 155–161.

Austin, N.L., Carter, R.T., & Vaux, A. (1990). The role of racial identity in Black students' attitudes toward counseling and counseling centers. *Journal of College Student Development, 31,* 237–244.

Backstrom, C.H., & Hursh, G.D. (1963). *Survey research.* Evanston, IL: Northwestern University Press.

Baker, F.M. (1988). Afro-Americans. In L. Comas-Diaz & E.E.H. Griffith (Eds.), *Clinical guidelines in cross-cultural mental health* (pp. 151–181). New York: John Wiley and Sons.

Baldwin, J.A. (1981). Notes on Africentric theory of Black personality. *The Western Journal of Black Studies, 5,* 172–179.

Baldwin, J.A. (1985). *African (Black) personality: From an Africentric framework.* Chicago: Third World Press.

Baldwin, J.A., & Bell, Y.R. (1985). The African Self-Consciousness scale: An Africentric personality questionnaire. *The Western Journal of Black Studies, 9,* 61–68.

Banks, J.A. (1984). Black youths in predominantly White suburbs: An exploratory study of their attitudes and self-concepts. *Journal of Negro Education, 53* (1), 3–17.

Barak, A., & LaCrosse, M.B. (1975). Multidimensional perception of counselor behavior. *Journal of Counseling Psychology, 22,* 471–476.

Baratz, S., & Baratz, J. (1970). Early childhood intervention: The social sciences base of institutional racism. *Harvard Educational Review, 40,* 29–50.

Beale, A.V. (1986). A cross-cultural dyadic encounter. *Journal of Multicultural Counseling and Development, 14,* 73–76.

Benesch, K.F., & Ponterotto, J.G. (1989). East and west: Transpersonal psychology and cross-cultural counseling. *Counseling and Values, 33,* 121–131.

Berg, J.H., & Wright, B. (1988). Effects of racial similarity and interviewer intimacy in a peer counseling analogy. *Journal of Counseling Psychology, 35,* 377–384.

Bernstein, B.L., Wade, P., & Hoffmann, B. (1987). Students' race and preferences for counselor's race, sex, age, and experience. *Journal of Multicultural Counseling and Development, 15,* 60–70.

Berry, J.W., & Kim, U. (1988). Acculturation and mental health. In P.R. Dasen, J.W. Berry, & N. Sartorius (Eds.), *Health and cross-cultural psychology: Toward applications* (pp. 207–236). Newbury Park, CA: Sage Publications.

Beyard-Tyler, K.C., & Haring, M.J. (1984). Navajo students respond to nontraditional occupations. Less information, less bias? *Journal of Counseling Psychology, 31,* 270–273.

Bickman, L. (1987). Graduate education in psychology. *American Psychologist, 42,* 1041–1047.

Bishop, J.B., & Richards, T.F. (1987). Counselor intake judgements about White and Black clients in a university counseling center. *Journal of Counseling Psychology, 34,* 96–98.

Blau, T. (1970). APA commission on accelerating Black participation in psychology. *American Psychologist, 25,* 1103–1104.

Boas, F. (1911). *Handbook of American Indian languages.* Washington, DC: Bureau of American Ethnology, Bulletin 40.

Bogdan, R.C., & Biklen, S.K. (1982). *Qualitative research for education: An introduction to theory and methods.* Boston: Allyn and Bacon, Inc.

Brandell, J.R. (1988). Treatment of the biracial child: Theoretical and clinical issues. *Journal of Multicultural Counseling and Development, 16,* 176–187.

Brewer, J., & Hunter, A. (1989). *Multimethod research: A synthesis of styles.* Newbury Park, CA: Sage Publications.

Briggs, C.L. (1986). *Learning how to ask: A sociolinguistic appraisal of the role of the interview in social science research.* Cambridge, MA: Cambridge University Press.

Brislin, R.W. (1970). Back-translation for cross-cultural research. *Journal of Cross-Cultural Psychology, 1,* 185–216.

Brislin, R.W. (1981). *Cross-cultural encounters: Face to face interaction.* New York: Pergamon.

Brislin, R.W. (1986). The wording and translation of research instruments. In W.J. Lonner & J.W. Berry (Eds.), *Field methods in cross-cultural research* (pp. 137–164). Beverly Hills, CA: Sage Publications.

Brislin, R.W., Lonner, W.J., & Thorndike, R.M. (1973). *Cross-cultural research methods.* New York: John Wiley and Sons.

Cameron, A.S., Galassi, J.P., Birk, J.M., & Waggener, N.M. (1989). Trends in counseling psychology training programs: The council of counseling psychology training programs survey, 1975–1987. *The Counseling Psychologist, 17,* 301–313.

Campbell, A. (1971). *White attitudes toward black people.* Ann Arbor: Institute for Social Research.

Campbell, D.T. (1967). Stereotypes and the perception of group differences. *American Psychologist, 22,* 817–829.

Carney, C.G., & Kahn, K.B. (1984). Building competencies for effective cross-cultural counseling: A developmental view. *The Counseling Psychologist, 12,* 111–119.

Carter, R.T. (1990a). Cultural value differences between African Americans and White Americans. *Journal of College Student Development, 31,* 71–79.

Carter, R.T. (1990b). Does race or racial identity attitudes influence the counseling process in Black and White dyads? In J.E. Helms (Ed.), *Black and White racial identity: Theory, research, and practice* (pp. 145–163). New York: Greenwood Press.

Carter, R.T., & Helms, J.E. (1990). White racial identity attitudes and cultural values. In J.E. Helms (Ed.), *Black and White racial identity: Theory, research, and practice* (pp. 105–118). New York: Greenwood Press.

Casas, J.M. (1976). Applicability of a behavioral model in serving the mental health needs of the Mexican American. In M.R. Miranda (Ed.), *Psychotherapy with the Spanish speaking: Issues in research and service delivery* (pp. 61–65). Los Angeles: Spanish-Speaking Mental Health Research Center.

Casas, J.M. (1984). Policy, training and research in counseling psychology: The racial/ethnic minority perspective. In S.D. Brown & R. Lent (Eds.), *Handbook of counseling psychology* (pp. 785–831). New York: John Wiley and Sons.

Casas, J.M. (1985a). A reflection on the status of racial/ethnic minority research. *The Counseling Psychologist, 13,* 581–598.

Casas, J.M. (1985b). The status of racial- and ethnic-minority counseling: A training perspective. In P.B. Pedersen (Ed.), *Handbook of cross-cultural counseling and therapy* (pp. 267–274). Westport, CT: Grenwood Press.

Casas, J.M., & Furlong, M.J. (in press). Empowering Hispanic parents: Increasing school involvement. In J. Carey & P.B. Pedersen (Eds.), *Multicultural counseling in schools.* Boston: Allyn and Bacon.

Casas, J.M., & Ponterotto, J.G. (1984). Profiling an invisible minority in higher education: The Chicana. *Personnel and Guidance Journal, 62,* 349–353.

Casas, J.M., Ponterotto, J.G., & Gutierez, J.M. (1986). An ethical indictment of counseling research and training: The cross-cultural perspective. *Journal of Counseling and Development, 64, 347–349.*

Casas, J.M., & Thompson, C.E. (in press). Ethical principles and standards: A racial/ethnic minority research perspective. *Counseling and Values.*

Casas, J.M., & Vasquez, M.J.T. (1989). Counseling Hispanics. In P.B. Pedersen, W. Lonner, J. Draguns, & J.E. Trimble (Eds.), *Counseling across cultures* (3rd ed.) (pp. 153–176). Honolulu, HI: University of Hawaii Press.

Casas, J.M., Vasquez, M.J.T., Barón, A., & Ponterotto, J.G. (1991). *Casebook of cross-cultural counseling* [in preparation]. Newbury Park, CA: Sage Publications.

Cayleff, S.E. (1986). Ethical issues in counseling gender, race, and culturally distinct groups. *Journal of Counseling and Development, 64,* 345–347.

Cherbosque, J. (1987). Differences between Mexican and American clients in expectations about psychological counseling. *Journal of Multicultural Counseling and Development, 15,* 110–114.

Chikezie, E.A. (1984). Cross-cultural counseling concerns. *Personnel and Guidance Journal, 62,* 339–341.

Claiborn, C.D., LaFromboise, T.D., & Pomales, J. (1986). Cross-cultural counseling process research: A rejoinder. *Journal of Counseling Psychology, 33,* 220–221.

Claney, D., & Parker, W.M. (1989). Assessing white racial consciousness and perceived comfort with Black individuals: A preliminary study. *Journal of Counseling and Development, 67,* 449–451.

Clark, K. (1971, January). Editorial. *APA Monitor*, p. 2.

Clark, M.L., Windley, L., Jones, L., & Ellis, S. (1986). Dating patterns of Black students on White southern campuses. *Journal of Multicultural Counseling and Development, 14,* 85–93.

Cole, S.M., Thomas, A.R., & Lee, C.C. (1988). School counselor and school psychology: Partners in minority family outreach. *Journal of Multicultural Counseling and Development, 16,* 110–116.

Coley, S.M., & Beckett, J.O. (1988). Black battered women: A review of empirical literature. *Journal of Counseling and Development, 66,* 266–270.

Comas-Diaz, L. (in press). Ethnic minority mental health: Contributions and future directions of the American Psychological Association. In S.C. Serafica, A.I. Schwebel, R.K. Russell, P.D. Issac, & L.B. Myers (Eds.), *Mental health of ethnic minorities.* New York: Praeger Press.

Comte, A. (1896). *The positive philosophy.* Translated by Harriet Martineau. London: George Bell and Sons.

Corsini, R.J., & Wedding, D. (Eds.). (1989). *Current psychotherapies* (4th ed.). Itasca, IL: Peacock Publishers.

Corvin, S.A., & Wiggins, F. (1989). An antiracism training model for white professionals. *Journal of Multicultural Counseling and Development, 17,* 105–114.

Cross, W.E., Jr. (1971). The negro-to-black conversion experience: Toward a psychology of black liberation. *Black World, 20,* 13–27.

Cross, W.E., Jr. (1978). The Cross and Thomas models of psychological nigrescence. *Journal of Black Psychology, 5,* 13–19.

Cross, W.E., Jr. (1987). A two-factor theory of Black identity: Implications for the study of identity development in minority children. In J.S. Phinney & M.J. Rotheram (Eds.), *Children's ethnic socialization: Pluralism and development* (pp. 117–133). Newbury Park, CA: Sage Publications.

Cross, W.E., Jr. (1989). Nigrescence: A nondiaphanous phenomenon. *The Counseling Psychologist, 17,* 273–276.

Cuellar, I., Harris, L.C., & Jasso, R. (1980). An acculturation scale for Mexican-American normal and clinical populations. *Hispanic Journal of Behavioral Sciences, 2,* 199–217.

d'Ardenne, P., & Mahtani, A. (1990). *Transcultural counseling in action.* London: Sage Publications.

Das, A.K. (1987). Indigenous models of therapy in traditional Asian societies. *Journal of Multicultural Counseling and Development, 15,* 25–37.

Denzin, N. (1978). *The research act: A theoretical introduction to sociological methods* (2nd ed.). New York: McGraw-Hill.

Deutscher, I. (1973). *What we say, what we do: Sentiments and acts.* Glenview, IL: Scott, Foresman.

Diaz-Guerrero, R. (1977). A Mexican psychology. *American Psychologist, 32,* 934–944.

Dillard, J.M. (1985). *Multicultural counseling: Toward ethnic and cultural relevance in human encounters.* Chicago: Nelson-Hall.

Dinges, N.G., Trimble, J.E., Manson, S.M., & Pasquale, F.L. (1981). Counseling and psychotherapy with American Indians and Alaskan Natives. In A.J. Marsella &

P.B. Pedersen (Eds.), *Cross-cultural counseling and psychotherapy* (pp. 243–276). New York: Pergamon Press.

Dominelli, L. (1988). *Anti-racist social work.* London: Macmillan Education.

Draguns, J.G. (1974). Values reflected in psychopathology: The case of the Protestant ethic. *Ethos, 2,* 115–136.

Durkheim, E. (1938). *The rules of sociological method.* New York: Free Press.

Durkheim, E. (1951). *Suicide: A study of sociology.* Translated and edited by George Simpson. New York: Free Press.

Esquivel, G.B., Keitel, M.A. (1990). Counseling immigrant children in the schools. *Elementary School Guidance and Counseling Journal, 24,* 213–221.

Fine, G.A., & Sandstrom, K.L. (1988). *Knowing children: Participant observation with minors.* Qualitative Research Methods, Volume 15. Newbury Park, CA: Sage Publications.

Fielding, N.G., & Fielding, J.L. (1986). *Linking data.* Qualitative Research Methods, Volume 4. Newbury Park, CA: Sage Publications.

Folensbee, R.W., Jr., Draguns, J.G., & Danish, S.J. (1986). Impact of two types of counselor intervention on Black American, Puerto Rican, and Anglo-American analogue clients. *Journal of Counseling Psychology, 33,* 446–453.

Forbes, J.D. (1988). Undercounting Native Americans: The 1980 census and the manipulation of racial identity in the United States. *Storia Nordamericana, 5,* (Torino, Italy), 1–35.

Foster, W., & Seltzer, A. (1986). A portrayal of individual excellence in the urban ghetto. *Journal of Counseling and Development, 64,* 579–582.

Fouad, N.A., Cudeck, R., & Hansen, J.C. (1984). Convergent validity of the Spanish and English forms of the Strong-Campbell Interest Inventory for bilingual Hispanic high school students. *Journal of Counseling Psychology, 31,* 339–348.

Francis, K.C., & Kelly, R.J. (1988). Female SEEK students: A study of status and academic performance. *Journal of Multicultural Counseling and Development, 16,* 165–175.

Fukuyama, M.A., & Greenfield, T.K. (1983). Dimensions of assertiveness in an Asian American student population. *Journal of Counseling Psychology, 30,* 429–432.

Gade, E.M., Fuqua, D., & Hurlburt, G. (1984). Use of Self-Directed Search with Native American high school students. *Journal of Counseling Psychology, 31,* 584–587.

Gade, E., Fuqua, D., & Hurlburt, G. (1988). The relationship of Holland's personal types to educational satisfaction with a Native-American high school population. *Journal of Counseling Psychology, 35,* 183–186.

Gade, E., & Hurlburt, G. (1985). Personality characteristics of female, American Indian alcoholics: Implications for counseling. *Journal of Multicultural Counseling and Development, 13,* 170–175.

Gallessich, J., & Olmstead, K.M. (1987). Training in counseling psychology: Issues and trends in 1986. *The Counseling Psychologist, 15,* 596–600.

Gardner, W.E. (1985). Hope: A factor in actualizing the young adult Black male. *Journal of Multicultural Counseling and Development, 13,* 130–136.

Garrison, S., & Jenkins, J.O. (1986). Differing perceptions of Black assertiveness as a function of race. *Journal of Multicultural Counseling and Development, 14,* 157–166.

Gary, L.E., & Berry, G.L. (1985). Depressive symptomatology among Black men. *Journal of Multicultural Counseling and Development, 13,* 121–129.

Gazda, G.M., Asburry, F.R., Balzea, F.J., Childers, W.C., & Walters, R.D. (1977). *Human relations development* (2nd. ed.). Boston: Allyn & Bacon.

Gazda, G.M., Rude, S.S., & Weissberg, M. (Eds.). (1988). Third national conference for counseling psychology: Planning the future [Special issue]. *The Counseling Psychologist, 16* (3).

Gelso, C.J. (1979). Research in counseling: Methodological and professional issues. *The Counseling Psychologist, 8,* 7–36.

Gelso, C.J., Betz, N.E., Friedlander, M.L., Helms, J.E., Hill, C.E., Patton, M.J., Super, D.E., & Wampold, B.E. (1988). Research in counseling psychology: Prospects and recommendations. *The Counseling Psychologist, 16,* 385–406.

George, V.D. (1986). Talented adolescent women and the motive to avoid success. *Journal of Multicultural Counseling and Development, 14,* 132–139.

Gephart, R.P., Jr. (1988). *Ethnostatistics: Qualitative foundations for quantitative research.* Qualitative Research Methods, Volume 12. Newbury Park, CA: Sage Publications.

Gibbs, J.T., & Huang, L.N. (1989a). A conceptual framework for assessing and treating minority youth. In J.T. Gibbs & L.N. Huang (Eds.), *Children of color: Psychological interventions with minority youth* (pp. 1–29). San Francisco: Jossey-Bass.

Gibbs, J.T., & Huang, L.N. (Eds.). (1989b). *Children of color: Psychological intervention with minority youth.* San Francisco: Jossey-Bass.

Giles, H.C. (1990). Counseling Haitian students and their families: Issues and interventions. *Journal of Counseling and Development, 68,* 317–320.

Gilligan, C. (1982). *In a different voice.* Cambridge, MA: Harvard University Press.

Goldman, L. (1976). A revolution in counseling research. *Journal of Counseling Psychology, 23,* 543–552.

Goldman, L. (1977). Toward more meaningful research. *Personnel and Guidance Journal, 55,* 363–368.

Goldman, L. (Ed.). (1978). *Research methods for counselors: Practical approaches in field settings.* New York: John Wiley and Sons.

Goldman, L. (1989). Moving counseling research into the 21st century. *The Counseling Psychologist, 17,* 81–85.

Gordon, M., & Grantham, R.J. (1979). Helper preferences in disadvantaged students. *Journal of Counseling Psychology, 26,* 337–343.

Gordon, M.M. (1964). *Assimilation in American life.* New York: Oxford University Press.

Gordon, T. (1973). Notes on White and Black psychology. *Journal of Social Issues, 29* (1), 87–95.

Grace, C. (1984). *The relationship between racial identity attitudes and choices of typical and atypical occupations among black college students.* Unpublished doctoral dissertation, Teachers College, Columbia University, New York.

Greeley, A.M., & Sheatsley, P.B. (1971). Attitudes toward racial integration. *Scientific American, 225,* 13–19.

Green, C.F., Cunningham, J., & Yanico, B.J. (1986). Effects of counselor and subject race and counselor physical attractiveness on impressions and expectations of a female counselor. *Journal of Counseling Psychology, 33,* 349–352.

Gregory, S., & Lee, S. (1986). Psychoeducational assessment of racial and ethnic minority groups: Professional implications. *Journal of Counseling and Development, 64,* 635–637.

Gubrium, J.F., & Silverman, D. (1989). *The politics of field research: Sociology beyond enlightenment.* London: Sage Publications.

Gunnings, T.S., & Lipscomb, W.D. (1986). Psychotherapy for Black men: A systemic approach. *Journal of Multicultural Counseling and Development, 14,* 17–24.

Guthrie, G.M., & Lonner, W.J. (1986). Assessment of personality and psychopatholopgy. In W.J. Lonner & J.W. Berry (Eds.), *Field methods in cross-cultural research* (pp. 231–264). Newbury Park, CA: Sage Publications.

Hall, W.S., Cross, W.E., & Freedle, R. (1972). Stages in the development of black awareness: An empirical investigation. In R.L. Jones (Ed.), *Black psychology* (pp. 156–165). New York: Harper & Row.

Halleck, S.L. (1971). Therapy is the handmaiden of the status quo. *Psychology Today, 4,* 30–34, 98–100.

Harding, S. (1987). The curious coincidence of feminine and African moralities: Challenges for feminist theory. In E.F. kittay & D.T. Meyers (Eds.), *Women and moral theory* (pp. 296–315). Totowa, NJ: Rowman and Littlefield.

Haviland, M.G., Horswill, R.K., O'Connell, J.T., & Dynneson, V.V. (1983). Native American college students' preference for counselor race and sex and the likelihood of their use of a counseling center. *Journal of Counseling Psychology, 30,* 267–270.

Heath, A.E., Neimeyer, G.J., & Pedersen, P.B. (1988). The future of cross-cultural counseling: A Delphi poll. *Journal of Counseling and Development, 67,* 27–30.

Helms, J.E. (1984). Toward a theoretical model of the effects of race on counseling: A black and white model. *The Counseling Psychologist, 12,* 153–165.

Helms, J.E. (1986). Expanding racial identity theory to cover counseling process. *Journal of Counseling Psychology, 33,* 62–64.

Helms, J.E. (1989a). At long last—Paradigms for cultural psychology research. *The Counseling Psychologist, 17,* 98–101.

Helms, J.E. (1989b). Considering some methodological issues in racial identity counseling research. *The Counseling Psychologist, 17,* 227–252.

Helms, J.E. (1989c). Eurocentricism strikes in strange ways and in unusual places. *The Counseling Psychologist, 17,* 643–647.

Helms, J.E. (Ed.). (1990). *Black and white racial racial identity: Theory, research, and practice.* New York: Greenwood Press.

Helms, J.E., & Carter, R.T. (1990). Development of the White Racial Identity Inventory. In J.E. Helms (Ed.), *Black and white racial identity: Theory, research, and practice* (pp. 67–80). New York: Greenwood Press.

Helms, J.E., & Parham, T.A. (1990). Black Racial Identity Attitude Scale (Form RIAS–B). In J.E. Helms (Ed.), *Black and white racial identity: Theory, research, and practice* (pp. 245–247).

Helms, J.E., & Parham, T.A. (in press). The development of the racial identity attitude scale. In R.L. Jones (Ed.), *Handbook of tests and measurements for Black populations*, (Vols. 1–2). Berkeley, CA: Cobb & Henry.

Henkin, W.A. (1985). Toward counseling the Japanese in America: A cross-cultural primer. *Journal of Counseling and Development, 63*, 500–503.

Henry, P., Bardo, H.R., Mouro, J.T., & Bryson, S. (1987). Medicine as a career choice and Holland's theory: Do race and sex make a difference? *Journal of Multicultural Counseling and Development, 15*, 161–170.

Hernandez, A.G., & Kerr, B.A. (1985, August). *Evaluating the triad model and traditional cross-cultural counselor training.* Paper presented at the annual meeting of the American Psychological Association, Los Angeles, CA.

Hernandez, A.G., & LaFromboise, T.D. (1985, August). *The development of the Cross-Cultural Counseling Inventory.* Paper presented at the annual meeting of the American Psychological Association, Los Angeles, CA.

Herring, R.D. (1989). American-Native families: Dissolution by coercion. *Journal of Multicultural Counseling and Development, 17*, 4–13.

Herring, R.D. (1990). Understanding Native-American values: Process and content concerns for counselors. *Counseling and Values, 34*, 134–137.

Hersen, M., & Barlow, D.H. (1976). *Single-case experimental designs: Strategies for studying behavior change.* New York: Pergamon Press.

Hill, C.E., Carter, J., & O'Farrell, M.K. (1983). A case study of the process and outcome of time-limited counseling. *Journal of Counseling Psychology, 30*, 3–18.

Hillerbrand, E. (1987). Philosophical tensions influencing psychology and social action. *American Psychologist, 42*, 111–118.

Hills, H.I., & Strozier, A.L. (1990, February). *Multicultural training in APA-approved counseling psychology programs: A survey.* Paper presented at the 7th annual Winter Roundtable on Cross-Cultural Counseling and Psychotherapy, Teachers College, Columbia University, New York.

Ho, M.K. (1987). *Family therapy with ethnic minorities.* Newbury Park, CA: Sage Publications.

Hodgkinson, H.L. (1985). *All one system: Demographics of education, kindergarten through graduate school.* Washington, DC: Institute for Educational Leadership.

Hoffman, P.H., & Hale-Benson, P. (1987). Self-esteem of Black middle-class women who choose to work inside or outside the home. *Journal of Multicultural Counseling and Development, 15*, 71–80.

Hollis, J., & Wantz, R. (1986). *Counselor preparation programs: Personnel trends, 1985–1986.* Muncie, IN: Accelerated Development.

Hoshmand, L.L.S.T. (1989). Alternate research paradigms: A review and teaching proposal. *The Counseling Psychologist, 17*, 3–79.

Hsu, F.L.K. (Ed.). (1972). *Psychological anthropology* (2nd. ed.). Cambridge, MA: Schenkman.

Huey, W.C., & Rank, R.C. (1984). Effects of counselor and peer-led group assertive training on Black adolescent aggression. *Journal of Counseling Psychology, 31*, 95–98.

Husserl, E. (1913). *Ideas.* London: George Allen and Unwin.

Ibrahim, F.A., & Arredondo, P.M. (1986). Ethical standards for cross-cultural counseling: Counselor preparation, practice, assessment, and research. *Journal of Counseling and Development, 64,* 349–352.

Ibrahim, F.A., & Kahn, H. (1987). Assessment of world views. *Psychological Reports, 60,* 163–176.

Ibrahim, F.A., Stadler, H.A., Arredondo, P., & McFadden, J. (1986, April). *Status of human rights issues in counselor education: A national survey.* Paper presented at the annual meeting of the American Association for Counseling and Development, Los Angeles, CA.

Inouye, K.H., & Pedersen, P.B. (1985). Cultural and ethnic content of the 1977 to 1982 American Psychological Association convention programs. *The Counseling Psychologist, 13,* 639–648.

Ishiyama, F.I. (1987). Use of Morita therapy in shyness counseling in the West: Promoting the client's self-acceptance and action taking. *Journal of Counseling and Development, 65,* 547–551.

Itzkowitz, S.G., & Petrie, R.D. (1988). Northern Black urban college students and the revised Student Development Task Inventory. *Journal of Multicultural Counseling and Development, 16,* 63–72.

Ivey, A.E. (1987). The multicultural practice of therapy: Ethics, empathy, and dialectics. *Journal of Social and Clinical Psychology, 5,* 195–204.

Jackson, B. (1975). Black identity development. *MEFORM: Journal of Educational Diversity and Innovation, 2,* 19–25.

Jackson, J. (1987). Counseling as a strategy for mainstreaming underprepared students. *Journal of Multicultural Counseling and Development, 15,* 184–190.

Jaeger, R.M. (Ed.). (1988). *Complementary methods: For research in education.* Washington, DC: American Educational Research Association.

Jensen, A.R. (1969). How much can we boost IQ and scholastic achievement? *Harvard Educational Review, 39,* 1–123.

Johnson, M.E., & Brems, C. (1990). Psychiatric inpatient MMPI profiles: An exploration for potential racial bias. *Journal of Counseling Psychology, 37,* 213–215.

June, L.N. (1986). Enhancing the delivery of mental health and counseling services to Black males: Critical agency and provider responsibilities. *Journal of Multicultural Counseling and Development, 14,* 39–45.

Katz, J.H. (1977). The effects of a systematic training program on the attitudes and behavior of White people. *International Journal of Intercultural Relations, 1* (1), 77–89.

Katz, J.H. (1985). The sociopolitical nature of counseling. *The Counseling Psychologist, 13,* 615–624.

Katz, J.H., & Ivey, A. (1977). White awareness: The frontier of racism awareness training. *Personnel and Guidance Journal, 55,* 485–489.

Kirk, A.R. (1986). Destructive behaviors among members of the Black community with a special focus on males: Causes and methods of intervention. *Journal of Multicultural Counseling and Development, 14,* 3–9.

Kirk, J., & Miller, M.L. (1986). *Reliability and validity in qualitative research.* Qualitative Research Methods, Volume 1. Newbury Park, CA: Sage Publications.

Klockars, C.B. (1974). *The professional fence.* New York: Free Press.

Klockars, C.B. (1977). Field ethics for the life history. In R.S. Weppner (Ed.), *Street ethnography* (pp. 201–226). Beverly Hills, CA: Sage Publications.

Kluckholn, F.R., Strodtbeck, F.L. (1961). *Variations in value orientations.* Evanston, IL: Row, Peterson.

Korman, M. (1974). National conference on levels and patterns of professional training in psychology: Major themes. *American Psychologist, 29,* 301–313.

Krogman, W.M. (1945). The concept of race. In R. Linton (Ed.), *The science of man [women] in world crisis* (pp. 38–61). New York: Columbia University Press.

LaCrosse, M.B., & Barak, A. (1976). Differential perception of counselor behavior. *Journal of Counseling Psychology, 23,* 170–172.

LaFromboise, T.D. (1988). American Indian mental health policy. *American Psychologist, 43,* 388–397.

LaFromboise, T.D., Coleman, H.L.K., & Hernandez, A. (1990). *Development and factor structure of the Cross-Cultural Counseling Inventory-Revised.* Manuscript submitted for publication.

LaFromboise, T.D., & Foster, S.L. (1989). Ethics in multicultural counseling. In P.B. Pedersen, J.G. Draguns, W.J. Lonner, & J.E. Trimble (Eds.), *Counseling across cultures* (3rd ed.). (pp. 115–136). Honolulu, HI: University of Hawaii Press.

LaFromboise, T.D., & Low, K.G. (1989). American Indian children and adolescents. In J.T. Gibbs & L.N. Huang (Eds.), *Children of color: Psychological intervention with minority youth* (pp. 114–147). San Francisco: Jossey-Bass.

LaFromboise, T.D., & Rowe, W. (1983). Skills training for bicultural competence: Rationale and application. *Journal of Counseling Psychology, 30,* 589–595.

Larrabee, M.J. (1986). Helping reluctant Black males: An affirmative approach. *Journal of Multicultural Counseling and Development, 14,* 25–38.

Lee, C. (1989). Editorial: Who speaks for multicultural counseling? *Journal of Multicultural Counseling and Development, 17,* 1–3.

Lee, D.Y., Sutton, R., Honore, F., & Uhlemann, M. (1983). Effects of counselor race on perceived counseling effectiveness. *Journal of Multicultural Counseling and Development, 30,* 447–450.

Leonard, P.Y. (1985). Vocational theory and the vocational behavior of Black males: An analysis. *Journal of Multicultural Counseling and Development, 13,* 91–105.

Leong, F.T.L. (1986). Counseling and psychotherapy with Asian-Americans: Review of the literature. *Journal of Counseling Psychology, 33,* 196–206.

Liebow, E. (1967). *Tally's corner.* Boston: Little, Brown.

Lincoln, Y., & Guba, E. (1985). *Naturalistic inquiry.* Beverly Hills, CA: Sage Publications.

Lindstrom, R.R., & Van Sant, S. (1986). Special issues in working with gifted minority adolescents. *Journal of Counseling and Development, 64,* 583–586.

Linton, R. (Ed.). (1945). *The science of man [women] in the world crisis.* New York: Columbia University Press.

Lonner, W.J., & Berry, J.W. (Eds.). (1986). *Field methods in cross-cultural research.* Beverly Hills, CA: Sage Publications.

Lonner, W.J., & Ibrahim, F.A. (1989). Assessment in cross-cultural counseling. In P.B. Pedersen, J.G. Draguns, W.J. Lonner, & J..E. Trimble (Eds.), *Counseling across cultures* (3rd ed.) (pp. 299–334). Honolulu, HI: University of Hawaii Press.

Lonner, W.J., & Sundberg, N.D. (1985). Assessment in cross-cultural counseling and therapy. In P. Pedersen (Ed.), *Handbook of cross-cultural counseling and therapy* (pp. 195–205). Westport, CT: Greenwood Press.

Lunneburg, C.E., & Lunneburg, P.W. (1986). Beyond prediction: The challenge of minority achievement in higher education. *Journal of Multicultural Counseling and Development, 14,* 77–84.

Malgady, R.G., Rogler, L.H., & Costantino, G. (1987). Ethnocultural and linguistic bias in mental health evaluation of Hispanics. *American Psychologist, 42,* 228–234.

Malinowski, B. (1932). *Argonauts of the Western Pacific.* London: Routledge.

Manson, S.M. (Ed.). (1982). *New directions in prevention among American Indian and Alaska Native communities.* Portland, Oregon: Oregon Health Sciences University.

Manson, S.M., & Trimble, J.E. (1982). American Indian and Alasks Native communities: Past efforts, future inquiries. In L.R. Snowden (Ed.), *Reaching the underserved: mental health needs of neglected populations* (pp. 143–163). Beverly Hills, CA: Sage Publications.

Margolis, R.L., & Rungta, S.A. (1986). Training counselors for work with special populations: A second look. *Journal of Counseling and Development, 64,* 642–644.

Markides, K.S., & Mindel, C.H. (1987). *Aging and ethnicity.* Newbury Park, CA: Sage Publications.

Marme, M., & Retish, P. (1988). Transition to work: Case history of a refugee family. *Journal of Multicultural Counseling and Development, 16,* 137–144.

Marsella, A.J. (1980). Depressive experience and disorder across cultures. In H.C. Triandis & J.G. Draguns (Eds.), *Handbook of cross-cultural psychology: Vol. 6. Psychopathology* (pp. 237–289). Boston: Allyn & Bacon.

Marshall, C., & Rossman, G.B. (1989). *Designing qualitative research.* Newbury Park, CA: Sage Publications.

Mathews, B., & Paradise, L.V. (1988). Toward methodological diversity: Qualitative research approaches. *Journal of Mental Health Counseling, 10,* 225–234.

McConahay, J.B. (1982). Self-interest versus racial attitudes as correlates of anti-busing attitudes in Louisville: Is it the buses or is it the blacks? *Journal of Politics, 44,* 692–720.

McConahay, J.B. (1983). Modern racism and modern discrimination: The effects of race, racial attitudes, and context on simulated hiring decisions. *Personality and Social Psychology Bulletin, 9,* 551–558.

McConahay, J.B. (1986). Modern racism, ambivalence, and the Modern Racism Scale. In J.F. Dovidio & S.L. Gaertner (Eds.), *Prejudice, Discrimination, and Racism* (pp. 91–125). New York: Academic Press.

McConahay, J.B., & Hough, J.C. (1976). Symbolic racism. *Journal of Social Issues, 32,* 23–45.

McFadden, J., & Wilson, R. (1977). *Non-white academic training within counselor education, rehabilitation counseling and student personnel programs.* Unpublished manuscript.

McGoldrick, M., Pearce, J., & Giordano, J. (Eds.). (1982). *Ethnicity and family therapy.* New York: Guilford Press.

McIntyre, L.D., & Pernell, E. (1985). The impact of race on teacher recommendations for special education placement. *Journal of Multicultural Counseling and Development, 13,* 112–120.

McKenzie, V.M. (1986). Ethnographic findings on West Indian-American clients. *Journal of Counseling and Development, 65,* 40–44.

Merta, R.J., Ponterotto, J.G., & Brown, R.D. (1990). *A comparison of two directive counseling approaches for use with international students.* Manuscript submitted for publication.

Merta, R.J., Stringham, E.M., & Ponterotto, J.G. (1988). Simulating culture shock in counselor trainees: An experiential exercise for cross-cultural training. *Journal of Counseling and Development, 66,* 242–245.

Miles, M., & Huberman, A. (1984). *Qualitative data analysis.* Beverly Hills, CA: Sage Publications.

Miller, M.J. (1985). Analyzing client change graphically. *Journal of Counseling and Development, 63,* 491–494.

Milliones, J. (1980). Construction of a Black consciousness measure: Psychotherapeutic implications. *Psychotherapy: Theory, Research, and Practice, 17,* 175–182.

Molina, R.A., & Franco, J.N. (1986). Effects of administrator and participant sex and ethnicity on self-disclosure. *Journal of Counseling and Development, 65,* 160–162.

Moore, B.M. (1974). Cultural differences and counseling perspectives. *Texas Personnel and Guidance Association*

Moynihan, D.P. (1965). Employment, income and the ordeal of the Negro family. *Daedalus, 4,* 745–770.

Myers, R.A. (1982). Education and training: The next decade. *The Counseling Psychologist, 10,* 39–45.

Nagata, D.K. (1989). Japanese American children and adolescents. In J.T. Gibbs & L.N. (Eds.), *Children of color: Psychological interventions with minority youth* (pp. 67–113). San Francisco: Jossey-Bass.

National Council of La Raza (1987). Focus—The U.S. Hispanic population: 1987. *Education Network News, 6* (5), 1–12.

Neimeyer, G.J., Fukuyama, M.A., Bingham, R.P., Hall, L.E., & Mussenden, M.E. (1986). Training cross-cultural counselors: A comparison of the pro-counselor and anti-counselor triad models. *Journal of Counseling and Development, 64,* 437–439.

Neymeyer, G.J., & Gonzales, M. (1983). Duration, satisfaction, and perceived effectiveness of cross-cultural counseling. *Journal of Counseling Psychology, 30,* 91–95.

Nobles, W.W. (1989). Psychological nigrescence: An Afrocentric review. *The Counseling Psychologist, 17,* 253–257.

Noddings, N. (1984). *Caring: A feminine approach to ethics and moral education.* Berkeley, CA: University of California Press.

Noddings, N. (1986). Fidelity in teaching, teacher education and research for teaching. *Harvard Educational Review, 56,* 496–510.

Obleton, N.B. (1984). Career counseling Black women in a predominantly White coeducational university. *Personnel and Guidance Journal, 62,* 365–368.

One-Third of a Nation (1988). A report of the commission on minority participation in education and American life. Washington, DC: American Council on Education.

Osipow, S.H. (1983). *Theories of career development* (3rd ed.). Englewood Cliffs, NJ: Prentice-Hall, Inc.

Padilla, A.M. (Ed.). (1980). *Acculturation: Theory, models and some new findings.* Boulder, CO: Westview Press.

Padilla, A.M., & Carlos, M.L. (1974). *Measuring ethnicity among Mexican-Americans: A preliminary report on the self-identity of a Latino group.* Paper presented at the 15th Interamerican Congress of Psychology, Bogata, Columbia.

Padilla A.M., & Lindholm, K.J. (1984). Hispanic behavioral science research: Recommendations for future research. *Hispanic Journal of Behavioral Sciences, 6,* 13–22.

Padilla, A.M., & DeSnyder, N.S. (1985). Counseling Hispanics: Strategies for effective interaction. In P.B. Pedersen (Ed.), *Handbook of cross-cultural counseling and therapy* (pp. 157–164). Westport, CT: Greenwood Press.

Palacios, M., & Franco, J.N. (1986). Counseling Mexican American women. *Journal of Multicultural Counseling and Development, 14,* 124–131.

Parham, T.A. (1989). Cycles of psychological nigrescence. *The Counseling Psychologist, 17,* 187–226.

Parham, T.A. & Helms, J.E. (1981). The influence of black students' racial attitudes on preferences for counselor's race. *Journal of Counseling Psychology, 28,* 250–257.

Parham, T.A. & Helms, J.E. (1985a). Attitudes of racial identity and self-esteem of black students: An exploratory investigation. *Journal of College Student Development, 26,* 143–147.

Parham, T.A. & Helms, J.E. (1985b). Relation of racial identity attitudes to self-actualization and affective states in black students. *Journal of Counseling Psychology, 32,* 431–440.

Parham, T.A., & McDavis, R.J. (1987). Black men, an endangered species: Who's really pulling the trigger? *Journal of Counseling and Development, 66,* 24–27.

Parker, W.M. (1988). *Consciousness-raising: A primer for multicultural counseling.* Springfield, IL: Charles C Thomas.

Patterson, C.H. (1972). Psychology and social responsibility. *Professional Psychology, 3,* 3–10.

Patterson, C.H. (1978). Cross-cultural or intercultural counseling or psychotherapy. *International Journal for the Advancement of Counselling, 1,* 231–247.

Patton, R. (1980). *Qualitative evaluation methods.* Beverly Hills, CA: Sage Publications.

Pearson, C.S., Shavlik, D.L., Touchton, J.G. (Eds.). (1989). *Educating the majority: Women challenge tradition in higher education.* New York: American Council on Education and Macmillan Publishing Company.

Pedersen, P.B. (1978). Four dimensions of cross-cultural skill in counselor training. *Personnel and Guidance Journal, 56,* 480–483.

Pedersen, P.B. (1979). Non-Western psychologies: The search for alternatives. In A.J. Marsella, R. Tharp, & T. Ciborowski (Eds.), *Perspectives in cross-cultural psychology* (pp. 77–98). New York: Academic Press.

Pedersen, P.B. (1983). Intercultural training of mental health providers. In D. Landis & R.W. Brislin (Eds.), *Handbook of intercultural training (Volume II): Issues in training methodology* (pp. 325–352). New York: Pergamon.

Pedersen, P.B. (Ed.). (1985). *Handbook of cross-cultural counseling and therapy.* Westport, CT: Greenwood Press.

Pedersen, P.B. (1986). The cultural role of conceptual and contextual support systems in counseling. *Journal of the American Mental Health Counselor's Association, 8,* 35–42.

Pedersen, P.B. (1987). Ten frequent assumptions of cultural bias in counseling. *Journal of Multicultural Counseling and Development, 15,* 16–24.

Pedersen, P.B. (1988). *A handbook for developing multicultural awareness.* Alexandria, VA: American Association for Counseling and Development.

Pedersen, P.B. (1990). The constructs of complexity and balance in multicultural counseling theory and practice. *Journal of Counseling and Development, 68,* 550–554.

Pedersen, P.B., Draguns, J.G., Lonner, W.L., & Trimble, J.E. (Eds.). (1989). *Counseling across cultures* (3rd ed.). Honolulu, HI: University of Hawaii Press.

Pedersen, P.B., & Ivey, A.E. (1987). Draft recommendations for changes in the APA ethical principles. *Internationally Speaking, 12,* 37–38.

Pedersen, P.B., & Marsella, A.J. (1982). The ethical crisis for cross-cultural counseling and therapy. *Professional Psychology, 13,* 492–500.

Pedigo, J. (1983). Finding the meaning of Native American substance abuse: Implications for community prevention. *Personnel and Guidance Journal, 61,* 273–277.

Perry, J.L., & Locke, D.C. (1985). Career development of Black men: Implications for school guidance services. *Journal of Multicultural Counseling and Development, 13,* 106–111.

Phllips, D., & Rathwell, T. (Eds.). (1986). *Health, race and ethnicity.* London: Croom Helm.

Pomales, J., Claiborn, C.D., & LaFromboise, T.D. (1986). Effects of black students' racial identity on perceptions of White counselors varying in cultural sensitivity. *Journal of Counseling Psychology, 33,* 57–61.

Ponce, F.Q., & Atkinson, D.R. (1989). Mexican-American acculturation, counselor ethnicity, counseling style, and perceived counselor credibility. *Journal of Counseling Psychology, 36,* 203–208.

Ponterotto, J.G. (1986). A content analysis of the *Journal of Multicultural Counseling and Development. Journal of Multicultural Counseling and Development, 14,* 98–107.

Ponterotto, J.G. (1987). Counseling Mexican-Americans: A multimodal approach. *Journal of Counseling and Development, 65,* 308–312.

Ponterotto, J.G. (1988a). Racial consciousness development among white counselor trainees: A stage model. *Journal of Multicultural Counseling and Development, 16,* 146–156.

Ponterotto, J.G. (1988b). Racial/ethnic minority research in the *Journal of Counseling Psychology:* A content analysis and methodological critique. *Journal of Counseling Psychology, 35,* 410–418.

Ponterotto, J.G. (1989). Expanding directions for racial identity research. *The Counseling Psychologist, 17,* 264–272.

Ponterotto, J.G. (in press a). Affirmative action: Current status and future needs. In J.G. Ponterotto, D.E. Lew, & R. Bullington (Eds.), *Affirmative action on campus.* New Directions for Student Services, No. 52. San Francisco: Jossey-Bass.

Ponterotto, J.G. (in press b). Racial/ethnic minority and women administrators and faculty in higher education: A status report. In J.G. Ponterotto, D.E. Lew, & R. Bullington (Eds.), *Affirmative action on campus.* New Directions for Student Services, No. 52. San Francisco: Jossey-Bass.

Ponterotto, J.G. (in press c). Racial/ethnic minority and women students in higher education: A status report. In J.G. Ponterotto, D.E. Lew, & R. Bullington (Eds.), *Affirmative action on campus.* New Directions for Student services, No. 52. San Francisco: Jossey-Bass.

Ponterotto, J.G., Alexander, C.M., & Hinkston, J.A. (1988). Afro-American preferences for counselor characteristics: A replication and extension. *Journal of Counseling Psychology, 35,* 175–182.

Ponterotto, J.G., Anderson, W.H., & Grieger, I. (1986). Black students' attitudes toward counseling as a function of racial identity. *Journal of Multicultural Counseling and Development, 14,* 50–59.

Ponterotto, J.G., Atkinson, D.R., Casas, J.M. Oda, A., & Pedersen, P.B. (1987, August). *In search of multicultural competence in counseling psychology programs.* Symposium presented at the annual meeting of the American Psychological Association, New York.

Ponterotto, J.G., & Benesch, K.F. (1988). An organizational framework for understanding the role of culture in counseling. *Journal of Counseling and Development, 66,* 237–241.

Ponterotto, J.G., & Casas, J.M. (1987). In search of multicultural competence within counselor education programs. *Journal of Counseling and Development, 65,* 430–434.

Ponterotto, J.G., Casas, J.M., Helms, J.E., Ivey, A., Parham, T.A., Pedersen, P.B., Sue, D.W. (1990, August). *The white American researcher in multicultural counseling: Significance, challenges, and rewards.* Symposium presented at the annual meeting of the American Psychological Association, Boston.

Ponterotto, J.G., & Furlong, M.J. (1985). Evaluating counselor effectiveness: A critical review of rating scale instruments. *Journal of Counseling Psychology, 32,* 597–616.

Ponterotto, J.G., Lew, D.E., & Bullington, R. (Eds.). (in press). *Affirmative action on campus.* New Directions for Student Services, No. 52. San Francisco: Jossey-Bass.

Ponterotto, J.G., & Merta, R.J. (1987). Peer counselors and international students: A field-based study. *Journal of International Student Personnel, 3* (2), 32–38.

Ponterotto, J.G., & Sabnani, H.B. (1989). "Classics" in multicultural counseling: A systematic five-year content analysis. *Journal of Multicultural Counseling and Development, 17,* 23–37.

Ponterotto, J.G., Sanchez, C., & Magids, D. (1990). *Development and initial validation of the Multicultural Counseling Awareness Scale (MCAS): Form A—Self Assessment.* Manuscript in preparation.

Ponterotto, J.G., & Wise, S.L. (1987). Construct validity study of the Racial Identity Attitude Scale. *Journal of Counseling Psychology, 34,* 218–223.

Ponterotto, J.G., Yoshida, R.K., Cancelli, A., Mendez, G., & Wasilewski, L. (1990). *Prospective minority graduate students perceptions of doctoral application materials: A qualitative study.* Manuscript in preparation.

Pope, B.R. (1986). Black men in interracial relationships. Psychological and thera-peutic issues. *Journal of Multicultural Counseling and Development, 14,* 10–16.

President's Commission on Mental Health (1978). *Task panel report to the president* (Vol. 1–4). Washington, DC: U.S. Government Printing Office.

Ramirez, M., Cox, B., & Castenada, A. (1977). *The psychodynamics of biculturalism.* Santa Cruz, CA: Systems and Evaluations in Education.

Reeder, B.L., & Heppner, P.P. (1985). Personal problem-solving activities of Black university students. *Journal of Multicultural Counseling and Development, 13,* 154–163.

Reisman, B.L., & Banuelos, D. (1984). Career fantasy in the barrio. *Journal of Non-White Concerns in Personnel and Guidance, 12,* 99–104.

Richardson, M.S., & Massey, J.P. (1986). Training programs in counseling psychology: 1984 data and trends. *The Counseling Psychologist, 14,* 313–318.

Richardson, R.C., Jr., & Bender, L.W. (1987). *Fostering minority access and achievement in higher education.* San Francisco: Jossey-Bass.

Rodriguez, M., & Blocher, D. (1988). A comparison of two approaches to enhancing career maturity in Puerto Rican college women. *Journal of Counseling Psychology, 35,* 275–280.

Rogler, L.H., Malgady, R.G., Costantino, G., & Blumenthal, R. (1987). What do culturally sensitive mental health services mean? The case of Hispanics. *American Psychologist, 42,* 565–570.

Rose, P.I. (1964). *They and we: Racial and ethnic relations in the United States.* New York: Random House.

Ross, D.B. (1984). A cross-cultural comparison of adult development. *Personnel and Guidance Journal, 62,* 418–421.

Rosser-Hogan, R. (1990). Making counseling culturally appropriate: Intervention with a Montagnard refugee. *Journal of Counseling and Development, 68,* 443–445.

Rotenberg, M. (1974). The Protestant ethic versus people-changing sciences. In J. Dawson & W.J. Lonner (Eds.), *Readings in cross-cultural psychology* (pp. 57–86). Hong Kong: University of Hong Kong Press.

Rude, S.S., Weissberg, M., & Gazda, G.M. (1988). Themes from the third national conference for counseling psychology. *The Counseling Psychologist, 16,* 423–430.

Rowe, D. (1988). *Stages of development for cross-culturally effective counselors.* Manuscript submitted for publication.

Sabnani, H.B., & Ponterotto, J.G. (1990, August). *Racial/ethnic minority instrumenta-tion in counseling research: A review, critique, and recommendations.* Paper presented at the annual meeting of the American Psychological Association, Boston, MA.

Sabnani, H.B., Ponterotto, J.G., & Borodovsky, L.G. (in press). White racial identity development and cross-cultural counselor training: A stage model. *The Counseling Psychologist.*

Sampson, E. (1977). Psychology and the American ideal. *Journal of Personality and Social Psychology, 11,* 767–782.

Sanchez, A.R., & Atkinson, D.R. (1983). Mexican-American cultural commitment, preference for counselor ethnicity, and willingness to utilize counseling. *Journal of Counseling Psychology, 30,* 215–220.

Sanders, D. (1987). Cultural conflicts: An important factor in the academic failures of American Indian students. *Journal of Multicultural Counseling and Development,* *15,* 81–90.

Scherman, A., & Doan, R.E., Jr. (1985). Subjects, designs, and generalizations in Volumes 25–29 of the *Journal of Counseling Psychology. Journal of Counseling Psychology, 32,* 272–276.

Schinke, S.P., Botvin, G.J., Trimble, J.E., Orlandi, L.D., Gilchrest, L.D., & Locklear, V.S. (1988). Preventing substance abuse among American-Indian adolescents: A bicultural competence skills approach. *Journal of Counseling Psychology, 35,* 87–90.

Schofield, J.W., & Anderson, K. (1987). Combining quantitative and qualitative components of research on ethnic identity and intergroup relations. In J.S. Phinney & M.J. Rotheram (Eds.), *Children's ethnic socialization: Pluralism and development* (pp. 252–273). Newbury Park, CA: Sage Publications.

Schuman, H., & Harding, J. (1963). Sympathetic identification with the underdog. *Public Opinion Quarterly, 27,* 230–241.

"Sex, Race/Ethnicity Data in Survey..." (1988). *Chronicle of Higher Education, 19* (11), p. 40.

Sheffey, M.A., Bingham, R.P., & Walsh, W.B. (1986). Concurrent validity of Holland's theory for college-educated Black men. *Journal of Multicultural Counseling and Development, 14,* 149–156.

Shipp, P.L. (1983). Counseling Blacks: A group approach. *Personnel and Guidance Journal, 62,* 108–111.

Shockley, W. (1971). *Journal of Law and Criminology, 7,* 530–543.

Shuey, A. (1966) *The testing of negro intelligence.* New York: Social Science Press.

Simpson, G.E., & Yinger, J.M. (1985). *Racial and cultural minorities: An analysis of prejudice and discrimination* (5th ed.). New York: Plenum Press.

Smith, A.L., & McMillon, H.G. (1986). Counselors as educational facilitators. *Journal of Multicultural Counseling and Development, 14,* 167–176.

Smith, E.M.J. (1977). Counseling Black individuals: Some stereotypes. *Personnel and Guidance Journal, 55,* 390–396.

Smith, E.M.J. (1989). Black racial identity development: Issues and concerns. *The Counseling Psychologist, 17,* 277–288.

Smith, E.M.J., & Vasquez, M.J.T. (Eds.). (1985). Cross-cultural counseling [Special issue]. *The Counseling Psychologist, 13* (4).

Smith, W.N., Burlew, A.K., Mosley, M.H. & Whitney, W.M. (1978). *Minority issues in mental health.* Reading, MA: Addison-Wesley.

Sodowsky, G.R., & Carey, J.C. (1988). Relationship between acculturation-related demographics and cultural attitudes of an Asian-Indian immigrant group. *Journal of Multicultural Counseling and Development, 16,* 117–136.

Sodowsky, G.R., & Taffe, R.C. (1990, February). [Initial] *Development and applications of the Multicultural Counseling Inventory.* Paper presented at the 7th annual Winter Roundtable on Cross-Cultural Counseling and Psychotherapy, Teachers College, Columbia University, New York.

Sodowsky, G.R., Taffe, R.C., & Gutkin, T. (1990). *Development and applications of the Multicultural Counseling Inventory.* Manuscript in preparation.

Stewart, E.C. (1972). *American cultural patterns: A cross-cultural perspective.* Yarmouth, ME: Intercultural Press.

Stewart, D., & Vaux, A. (1986). Social support resources, behaviors, and perceptions among Black and White college students. *Journal of Multicultural Counseling and Development, 14,* 65–72.

Stewart, D.A., & Benson, G. (1988). Dual cultural negligence: The education of Black deaf children. *Journal of Multicultural Counseling and Development, 16,* 98–109.

Stewart, G.G., & Lewis, W.A. (1986). Effects of assertiveness training on the self-esteem of Black high school students. *Journal of Counseling and Development, 64,* 638–641.

Strozier, A.L., & Hills, H.I. (1989, August). *Multicultural training in American Psycho — logical Association-approved counseling psychology programs: A survey.* Paper pre — sented at the annual meeting of the American Psychological Association, New Orleans.

Sue, D., Ino, S., & Sue, D.M. (1983). Nonassertiveness of Asian Americans: An inaccurate assumption? *Journal of Counseling Psychology, 30,* 581–588.

Sue, D.W. (1978). Eliminating cultural oppression in counseling: Toward a general theory. *Journal of Counseling Psychology, 25,* 419–428.

Sue, D.W. (1981). *Counseling the culturally different: Theory and practice.* New York: John Wiley and Sons.

Sue, D.W. (1989, August). Effective multicultural counseling: Proposed research directions. In N.A. Fouad (Chair), *Cross-cultural research and training: Focus on critical issues.* Symposium presented at the annual meeting of the American Psychological Association, New Orleans.

Sue, D.W., Bernier, J.E., Durran, A., Feinberg, L., Pedersen, P.B., Smith, E.J., & Vasquez-Nuttal, E. (1982). Position paper: Cross-cultural counseling competencies. *The Counseling Psychologist, 10,* 45–52.

Sue, D.W., & Sue, D. (1985). Asian-Americans and Pacific Islanders. In P.B. Pedersen (Ed.), *Handbook of cross-cultural counseling and therapy* (pp. 141–146). Westport, CT: Greenwood Press.

Sue, D.W., & Sue, D. (in press). *Counseling the culturally different: Theory and practice* (2nd. ed.). New York: John Wiley and Sons.

Sue, D.W. & Sue, S. (1972). Counseling Chinese Americans. *Personnel and Guidance Journal, 50,* 637–644.

Sue, S. (1981, April). *Ethnic minority issues in psychology: Something old and something new.* Paper presented at the annual meeting of the Western Psychological Association, Los Angeles, CA.

Sue, S. (1988). Psychotherapeutic services for ethnic minorities: Two decades of research findings. *American Psychologist, 43,* 301–308.

Sue, S., Akutsu, P.O., & Higashi, C. (1985). Training issues in conducting ther- apy with ethnic-minority-group clients. In P. Pedersen (Ed.), *Handbook of cross-cultural counseling and therapy* (pp. 275–280). Westport, CT: Greenwood Press.

Sue, S., & Zane, N.W. (1985). Academic achievement and socioeconomic adjustment among Chinese university students. *Journal of Counseling Psychology, 32,* 570–579.

Sue, S., & Zane, N.W. (1987). The role of culture and cultural techniques in psychotherapy: A critique and reformulation. *American Psychologist, 42,* 37–45.

Suinn, R.M. (1985). Research and practice in cross-cultural counseling. *The Counseling Psychologist, 13,* 673–684.

Szapocznik, J., Scopetta, M.A., Arnalde, M., & Kurtines, W. (1978). Cuban value structure: Treatment implications. *Journal of Consulting and Clinical Psychology, 46,* 961–970.

Szapocznik, J., Scopetta, M.A., Kurtines, W., Arnalde, M. (1978). Theory and measurement of acculturation. *Interamerican Journal of Psychology, 12,* 113–130.

Tapp, J.L., Kelman, H.C., Triandis, H.C., Wrightsman, L.S., & Coelho, G.V. (1974). Continuing concerns in cross-cultural ethics: A report. *International Journal of Psychology, 9,* 231–249.

Taussig, I.M. (1987). Comparative responses of Mexican Americans and Anglo Americans to early goal setting in a public mental health clinic. *Journal of Counseling Psychology, 34,* 214–217.

Taylor, S.J., & Bogdan, R. (1984). *Introduction to qualitative research methods: The search for meanings.* New York: John Wiley and Sons.

Terrell, F., & Terrell, S. (1981). An inventory to measure cultural mistrust among Blacks. *The Western Journal of Black Studies, 5,* 180–185.

Terrell, F., Terrell, S. (1984). Race of counselor, client sex, cultural mistrust level, and premature termination from counseling among Black clients. *Journal of Counseling Psychology, 31,* 371–375.

Terrell, F., & Miller, F.S. (1980). *The development of an inventory to measure experience with racialistic incidents among Blacks.* Unpublished manuscript.

Thomas, A., & Sillen, S. (1972). *Racism and psychiatry.* Secaucus, NJ: Citadel Press.

Thomas, C.W. (1970). Different strokes for different folks. *Psychology Today, 4,* 49–53, 80.

Thomas, C.W. (1971). *Boys no more.* Beverly Hills, CA: Glencoe Press.

Thomas, V.G. (1986). Career aspirations, Parental support, and work values among Black female adolescents. *Journal of Multicultural Counseling and Development, 14,* 177–185.

Thompson, C.E., Neville, H., Weathers, P.L., Poston, W.C., & Atkinson, D.R. (1990). Cultural mistrust and racism reaction among African-American students. *Journal of College Student Development, 31,* 162–168.

Thompson, E.T., & Hughes, E.C. (1958). *Race: Individual collective behavior.* Glencoe, IL: Free Press.

Thurman, P.J., Martin, D., & Martin, M. (1985). An assessment of attempted suicides among adolescent Cherokee Indians. *Journal of Non-White Concerns in Personnel and Guidance, 13,* 176–182.

Tidwell, R. (1988). The addition of counseling staff at racially isolated schools: An assessment by students and counselors. *Journal of Counseling and Development, 66,* 342–344.

Tomine, S. (1985). Jan Ken Po Gakko: A Japanese-American cultural education program. *Journal of Non-White Concerns in Personnel and Guidance, 13,* 164–175.

Tracey, T.J., Leong, F.T.L., & Glidden, C. (1986). Help seeking and problem perception among Asian Americans. *Journal of Counseling Psychology, 33,* 331–336.

U.S. Bureau of the Census (1980). *Population profile of the United States: 1980.* Population Characteristics (Series P-20, No. 363). Washington, DC: U.S. Government Printing Office.

U.S. Bureau of the Census (1980). *Population profile of the United States: 1980.* Population Characteristics (Series P-25, No. 952). Washington, DC: U.S. Government Printing Office.

U.S. Bureau of the Census (1987). *Statistical abstract of the United States: 1986* (107th ed.). Washington, DC: U.S. Government Printing Office.

U.S. Bureau of the Census (1988). *Statistical abstract of the United States: 1987* (108th ed.). Washington, DC: U.S. Government Printing Office.

U.S. Bureau of the Census (1988). *The Hispanic population in the United States: March, 1985.* Current Population Reports. Population Characteristics, Series P-20, No. 422. U.S. Government Printing Office.

U.S. Bureau of the Census (1989). *Statistical abstract of the United States: 1988* (109th ed.). Washington, DC: U.S. Government Printing Office.

U.S. Department of Commerce, Bureau of the Census. (May, 1983). *1980 census of population: Characteristics of the population* (U.S. Summary, PC 80-1-B1). Washington, DC: Author.

Van Maanen, J. (ed.). (1983). *Qualitative methodology.* Beverly Hills, CA: Sage Publications.

Vontress, C.E. (1988). An existential approach to cross0cultural counseling. *Journal of Multicultural Counseling and Development, 16,* 73–83.

Walsh, W.B., Woods, W.J., & Ward, C.M. (1986). Holland's theory and working Black and White women. *Journal of Multicultural Counseling and Development, 14,* 116–123.

Ward, J.V. (1990). Racial identity formation and transformation. In C. Gilligan, N.P. Lyons, & T.J. Hanmer (Eds.), *Making connections: The relational worlds of adolescent girls at Emma Willard School* (pp. 215–232). Cambridge, MA: Harvard University Press.

Wehrly, B., & Watson-Gegeo, K. (1985). Ethnographic methodologies as applied to the study of cross-cultural counseling. In P. B. Pedersen (Ed.), *Handbook of cross-cultural counseling and therapy* (pp. 65–71). Westport, CT: Greenwood Press.

Weissberg, M., Rude, S.S., Gazda, G., Bozarth, J.D., McDougal, K.S., Slavet, M.R., Smith, J.L., & Walsh, D.J. (1988). An overview of the third national conference for counseling psychology. *The Counseling Psychologist, 16,* 325–331.

White, J.L., & Parham, T.A. (1990). *Black psychology: An African-American perspective* (2nd. ed.). Englewood Cliffs, NJ: Prentice-Hall.

White, T.J., & Sedlacek, W.E. (1987). White student attitudes toward Blacks and Hispanics: Programming implications. *Journal of Multicultural Counseling and Development, 15,* 171–183.

Whiteley, J.M. (1984). Chapter 5: Alternative directions for the profession: The fifth historical period (1968–1976). *The Counseling Psychologist, 12,* 69–82.

Williams, R.L. (1981). *The collective Black mind: An Africentric theory of Black personality.* St. Louis: Williams & Associates.

Wilson, C.C., II., Gutierrez, F. (1985). *Minorities and media: Diversity and the end of mass communication.* Beverly Hills, CA: Sage Publications.

Wilson, R., & Justiz, M.J. (1987/1988). Minorities in higher education: Confronting a time bomb. *Educational Record, 68* (4) and *69* (1), 8–15.

Wirth, L. (1945). The problem of minority groups. In R. Linton (Ed.), *The science of man [woman] in the world crisis* (pp. 347–372). New York: Columbia University Press.

Wrenn, C.G. (1962). The culturally encapsulated counselor. *Harvard Educational Review, 32,* 444–449.

Wrenn, C.G. (1985). Afterward: The culturally encapsulated counselor revisited. In P.B. Pedersen (Ed.), *Handbook of cross-cultural counseling and therapy* (pp. 323–329). Westport, CT: Greenwood Press.

Wyatt, G.E., & Parham, W.D. (1985). The inclusion of culturally sensitive course materials in graduate school and training programs. *Psychotherapy, 22,* 461–468.

Yinger, J.M. (1976). Ethnicity in complex societies. In L.A. Coser & O.N. Larsen (Eds.), *The uses of controversy in sociology* (pp. 197–216). New York: Free Press.

Yoshida, R.K., Cancelli, A.A., Sowinski, J., & Bernhardt, R. (1989). Differences in information sent to minority and non-minority prospective applicants to clinical, counseling, and school psychology programs. *Professional Psychology: Research and Practice, 20,* 179–184.

Young, J.L. (1986). Developing nontraditional leaders. *Journal of Multicultural Counseling and Development, 14,* 108–115.

Zimmer, J. (1976). Concerning ecology in counseling. *Journal of Counseling Psychology, 25,* 225–230.

Zytowski, D.G., Casas, J.M., Gilbert, L.A., Lent, R.W., Simon, N.P. (1988). Counseling psychology's public image. *The Counseling Psychologist, 16,* 332–346.

AUTHOR INDEX

SUBJECT INDEX